NOBODY TOLD ME

love in the time of dementia

A MEMOIR

S.R. KARFELT

AMBERHORN

LIVONIA, MICHGAN

Book design by
Blue Harvest Creative
www.blueharvestcreative.com

NOBODY TOLD ME

Copyright © 2017 S.R. Karfelt

Published by Amber Horn
an imprint of BHC Press

Library of Congress Control Number:
2017933419

ISBN-13: 978-1-946006-62-2
ISBN-10: 1-946006-62-9

also available in eBook

Visit the author at:
www.SRKarfelt.com &
www.bhcpresss.com

ALSO BY S.R. KARFELT

The Covenant Keeper Novels
Kahtar—Warrior of the Ages
Heartless—A Shieldmaiden's Voice
Forever—The Constantines' Secret

Stand-alone Novels
Bitch Witch

Multi-author Collections
A Winter's Romance
In Creeps the Night
Through the Portal
Call of the Warrior

TABLE OF CONTENTS

AUTHOR'S NOTE

This is a true story. Some details are retrieved from long-term memory, but I rarely forget a good story. Exact wording eluded me in some instances, and since we all remember from our own perspective, I've included most dialogue without quotation marks. What I've written I can stand by comfortably. For the sake of privacy for my mother-in-law and others, I've used nicknames for most people and places.

Please keep in mind that I'm not a professional in dementia or the care of people with memory loss. I'm just a girl, standing in front of dementia, asking it WTF, like so many of you. The following is the story of how it answered me.

For those who've forgotten,
And those who cannot.

NOBODY
TOLD ME

HERE'S A GOOD IDEA

The last thing you want to do when you take your mother-in-law for a ride is to bring her to your house. "But we can't just dump her in some nursing home." That bit of commentary came from Juan, my husband of eighty billion years.

We were like-minded about that. We'd glanced at and rejected the pee-scented nursing homes closer to Gummy's house.

After millennia of marriage, I knew damn well how this was going to work. Especially since I've ditched our small engineering business to write full-time now. Everyone knows that writers are home all the time. They can watch your dogs. Get your kids off the bus. Wait for the cable guy. Having one in the neighborhood is a coup. Everyone wants one. You can make fun of their weird *and* get them to watch your mother who is exhibiting signs of dementia.

Consider this. Writers spend an inordinate amount of time researching how to hide a body. You've got a body. Try to keep that in mind. Just because we're introverts doesn't mean we're nice. We are not nice. Maybe we'll cooperate and help with your shit, but that's only because we're taking notes and fusing your freakiness into our stories. So watch out.

Oh, and by the way, it takes for-freaking-ever to write a flipping novel. Thus the reason the saying *'You don't have to write a novel'* is used when someone is taking way too long. Try it sometime. Sit down and pound out 80,000 words, then rework it so it isn't a steaming pile of *this makes no sense*. Good luck with that.

Even if we post to Twitter twenty times a day, it doesn't mean we're not busy.

Juan assured me that this would be different than every other thing since the dawn of our marriage. It was his mother and he'd take care of her. He'd take her to the doctor, and he'd start getting home from work on time—unlike the previous centuries of marriage. Even if the few last decades of his time had been eaten up by his engineering business, this would be different.

I'm only half as gullible as I look. The sun rises and sets every day; you start to expect things.

One thing about being married forever is you've had all the arguments. They've all been beaten down and driven over so many times they're like roadkill that's gone flat and unrecognizable, impossible to separate from the blacktop. There's no point in going over them again. They might be flat and done, but they still stink.

All those marital arguments get boring after a while. I'd taken to saying things like, "You know how I go on and on about how you have to break down your Amazon boxes before you put them into the recycling bin, because Jesus really isn't the one who comes along and flattens them for you every week? You know that rant? Do me a favor and replay that in your head right now, because the bin is full of intact boxes that need broken down, and I'm sick as shit of that one. Okay?"

That was my attitude about bringing Gummy here. I saw that train heading down the tracks in my direction. One time a neighbor used that metaphor for raising teenagers. I asked if I should run. She said only if I needed the exercise, because the train would catch up with me either way.

It was the same with Gummy.

16

chapter two

ARE WE THERE YET, HUH?

When the Anne Frank family left their home in Amsterdam to hide in the secret annex until World War II ended, they knew they wouldn't return. When I shanghaied Gummy out of her home of fifty years, she had no idea she'd never return.

I had my suspicions.

Hope just kept sitting on them.

Her memory problems were getting worse. She'd been getting lost. Misplacing grandchildren. Forgetting who was alive or dead. Getting confused about what she'd spent her day doing. Sometimes the truth caused a meltdown. The time had come for an intervention. I understood that.

I just didn't want to have it at my house.

However, we couldn't keep crossing state lines trying to take care of her and get her to doctors. She couldn't remember to take medicine. She couldn't remember if she had medicine to take. Heck, she couldn't remember if she had a doctor.

As fate would have it, the weekend we moved Gummy to our house, she was more animated and with it than she'd been in a long time. We went out to dinner and reminisced with family in her hometown, and when she climbed into the car she was on board with heading for our home in the shire. She wanted to see what the doctors there could do for her memory lapses. Both Juan and I had spent the weekend whispering back and forth, wondering if maybe we were jumping the gun. Maybe taking her home with us could wait another six months or a year.

In the end we decide that if nothing else, Gummy will get a checkup and good medical advice, and then we can take her back home.

Within the first hour I know Gummy isn't going back home. There is no way I am ever making this drive with her again. At this point, we don't know what the term *sundowning* means. All we know is Gummy morphed into something like a petulant four-year-old.

Now, where are we going?

To our house.

What? Why are we going clear to your house?

You're going to see the doctors there.

What are you talking about? I don't need to see a doctor. There's nothing wrong with me.

You have an appointment to have your memory checked.

Well, my memory is crap. Look at those hills! Where are we going?

Rinse and repeat.

For six hours. *Six hours.* Sure, you've probably had a ride like this with kids. I sure have. Here's the major difference. Even a four-year-old has rational moments. Okay, maybe not rational, but they occasionally visit the realm of logic. People with dementia don't, not when they're sundowning.

For six solid hours, on a nonstop loop, Gummy wonders where we are going. Every time the answer astonishes her. It is surprising how much energy a septuagenarian can have. After a few hours Juan and I are drooping. He tries to reason with her. He's a mad scientist. Logic is his friend. I, on the other hand, am a fiction writer. Nonsense doesn't upset me. I can cozy up to it. Any time I'm working on a book I spend months in a quagmire of gobble-dygook. It's not an uncomfortable place. This trip, however, none of us are anywhere near our comfort zone.

Gummy is an extrovert. I'm not. Being confined in the car with her while she runs in mental circles feels as though the life force is being drained from my body. Think empty gas tank, used up batteries, vampire has been here. I recognize her circular pattern. She did this at her house, but typically on a longer loop. For the last few years she's been hoarding, and at least once a day she'd latch onto some object. Once it was a filter from a vacuum cleaner she no longer had, or maybe never had. She spent hours walking around the house with it.

Do you see this?

What is it?

I'm not sure. I'm trying to figure that out.

It looks like a vacuum cleaner part.

Do you think so? Juan, do you see this?

I call it *sharking*. She would circle endlessly with whatever she'd caught. Sooner or later she set it down and we'd hide whatever it was to get a break from discussing the endless mystery of it.

Gummy sharked at night too, trying to figure out who was in her house. Let me take this moment to brag about my patience. I can devote myself unblinkingly to a task, novel writing, or conversation, but heaven help you if you wake me up or pester me in the morning. The way Gummy figured out who was at her house was to come into the room at night, flip the light on, and bend over the bed to have a good look. This never sat well with me.

Once satisfied, she'd head back out again, sometimes for a good ten minutes before she returned for another peek. There had been very lit-tle sleep our last couple visits. Last summer, she had it in her head it was

Halloween. A few preemptive ghost decorations were on display. That meant the air-conditioning had to be off too.

> It's too late in the year to have that on.
>
> *Gummy, it's ninety degrees*
>
> What? You know, I have been hot.
>
> *I'm going to turn on the air and cool it off in here.*
>
> I'm going to shut this off. It's too late in the year to have this on.

That visit we ended up sleeping in the living room under the lone ceiling fan, me on the sofa, Juan on the floor. He's chivalrous like that. The shark circled all night long, and if we fell asleep she'd helpfully shut off the ceiling fan so we wouldn't get cold.

During Gummy's circling, she'd also move our things. I'd spent an entire day searching for legal papers before we headed to her house with the intent to move her to ours. I went through every file in our house, searched vehicles, and went to the bank to dig through the safety deposit box—only to return home and look again. When we got to her house we found the missing paperwork in one of her drawers. She'd pilfered it last visit.

One visit half the clothing from my suitcase went missing. The appearance of a pair of men's jeans and an ancient yellowed article on the OJ Simpson trial told me what had happened. I thought maybe Gummy had discovered my suitcase, fell back in time to when her hubby lived, and repacked my suitcase thinking it was his. I have no idea about the newspaper clipping. She's always been a news hound, but I had no idea she'd started hoarding that long ago.

Here's the thing about my patience—I don't keep any reserves. When I run out it is gone. I'm done. I don't have the energy to get cranky. I'm peopled out and used up. A good hour before we reach our home in the shire I can't do it anymore. I close my eyes and droop in my seat.

That doesn't discourage Gummy. She keeps up her circular questioning.

Where are we going?

Why?

There's nothing wrong with me.

My memory is crap. Remind me where we're going.

Hey, where are we going?

Juan steps in, as I've slipped into an introvert coma over in the passenger seat. Focusing on the road, he had stopped responding. He has that engineer brain. Question? Answer. Needs? Met. Fact? Sure thing. Logic? You betcha. Illogical? He doesn't do illogical. His silence doesn't seem to bother Gum, but when I quit responding she forgets who I am. This is a first. We finally get to our house; Gummy doesn't ask where we are. She has other worries.

Who's that woman?

Mom, that's Saffi.

It is? You sure?

Yes, Mom, you know who that is. That's your daughter-in-law, Saffi.

She looks different.

chapter three

MEET THE IN-LAWS

The first time I met Gummy, she came running out of her house to smack her son.

She didn't say hello to me, too focused on yelling and whacking him around the head. We'd seen a movie a couple weeks earlier, and apparently Juan hadn't had the good sense not to recommend that his mother go see Porky's, one of those raunchy '80s teen flicks. And apparently she hadn't had the good sense not to take her entire church choir to go see it with her.

Juan and I had been dating a short time, but exclusively, and it was the mandatory meet-the-parents visit. That she might become my mother-in-law wasn't even an unconscious thought in my head. There were no plans for marriage in my imagination. Adventure wobbled around my field of vision, and being an adult in charge of my own destiny was all I wanted.

I first went out with Juan because of a palm reader. Not that I was into that mumbo jumbo; it'd happened during some event at the mall. She'd offered to read my hand for free, told me the birthdate of my soulmate and that the bulk of the information she needed was on my other hand, which she'd have to charge for. I've always been good at walking away when people disappoint me. So the rest of my future has remained a mystery.

Despite my skepticism, that birthdate stuck in my head. Not long afterward, paperwork for new hires came across my desk at work. Low and behold my soulmate had been hired. Isn't that incredibly convenient for me?

Despite my strict no dating coworkers policy, which was fairly easy to stick to since no one ever asked, I asked him out. It was at the cusp of that timeframe where most women still waited for the guy to ask her out, but I didn't have forever, people. Was the palm reader right or not? I needed to know! Juan had been trying to work up the nerve to ask me out since I showed up his first day in his first meeting (to scope him out). It obviously wasn't going to happen without some help. It's hard to believe now, but Juan used to be shy. So was I. I still am, but I don't like to waste time more.

That's also known as being impatient.

Was I just bragging about my patience? Ignore that.

I meant I *can* be patient. Intermittently. Part-time. Until I'm not.

After the first date, in which he didn't show up and I wrote him off, we were pretty much inseparable. Okay, technically he did show up, after midnight, covered in blood, with his arm in a sling. It was that old story, *my car caught fire in an underground garage and the thing you use to 'break glass in case of fire' was missing, so I had to use my fist to get the fire extinguisher. By the time the firemen came the tires had melted off my car, and I had to go to the hospital. I think I might need surgery on this hand. Could I borrow your car?*

If you've heard it once, you've heard it a million times.

But he was my soulmate after all, or at least, I really liked hanging out with him despite the self-fulfilling prophecy. I loaned him my car, and within a few weeks we went to meet the parents.

When Gummy took the time to take a good look at me, we were sitting together on her pretty flowered sofa, me between Juan and her. She hadn't seen him in a while, and they'd been catching up.

How was his job?

How was the drive?

23

Hey, his old girlfriend just stopped by the other day.

You know the pretty one with the impressive *chesticles*.

Sometimes I have to improvise on the exact words used. It's been a while. I assume you get the gist.

Sexy-exy still lived in his hometown. Unlike me. I was from far-far away, a land where Gummy's football rivals lived. This apparently did not bode well for my character. She pointed that out. I responded that I didn't follow football anyway. Wrong answer. I had a shitload of wrong answers. Still do. It's all I got, and at that time I definitely wasn't measuring up—not me or my subpar chesticles.

> Your socks don't match.

> *Oh. They never do.*

> What! Why not?

It's not a fashion statement. It's partially because one favorite sock is forever going astray, and partially because life is too damn short to match socks. I knew that even at a young age. Gummy, however, did not approve of my living-in-the-wrong-place, un-football-watching, unmatched-socks self.

Her disapproval had nothing to do with the fact that I later forced her son to fall in love with me and move even farther away. Moving was inevitable given his mad scientist profession. Nor did it have anything to do with my in-law motto: *Living far away from them is the key to a happy marriage.* She didn't even know about that motto, because I hadn't yet made it up.

Nope. She simply didn't care for me being with her son. Our compatibility isn't obvious, and as a mother myself now I understand. We're overprotective and assume we know what's best for our children. At the time I sensed how she felt and took it personally. This is how mothers-in-law and daughters-in-law often start their relationships. I didn't worry too much about it at the time. Maybe Juan was my soulmate, but I had adventures planned and Gummy didn't figure into my grand plans at all.

Or so I thought.

Have you ever visited someone who has a stinky dog you know, the kind that won't leave you alone? It stands about a foot from you, watching from the corner of its googly eyes, tongue dangling, with a doggy grin on its face. It'll scoot back toward you and use its head to flip your hand into proper petting position. You try to be polite with subliminal *scoot stinky dog!* body language. It won't go, and the owners are watching and waiting for you to succumb to the shedding, unwashed, *was that a flea?* hound they adore. Before you know it you're using your magical petting powers to scratch its ears so well it's drooling, and you even cave and rub the belly, knowing full-well you cannot use that hand for anything else until you wash it with plenty of antibacterial soap.

And now it wants to sit in your lap.

Uh-oh. Am I using a stinky dog that won't go away until you become friends with it as a *metaphor* for my in-laws? They didn't even have a dog, nor did they smell, and despite her dementia, when Gummy hears about this part of the book I am dog meat.

A man once griped to me at a funeral that his ex-wife wouldn't speak to him, even though it had been decades since his long list of crimes against her had been committed. I explained women to him. Why do some men complain that they don't understand women? Allow me to clear it up for you. It's very simple.

If it pissed us off *ever* in the history of the world, it still pisses us off. We are nothing if not consistent.

Might maybe have to get back to you on if the dog metaphor will eternally piss off your mother-in-law, despite the fact that she can't remember anything else. Based on the last billion years of my marriage and my observations of Gummy, I'd have to go with yes.

Might edit that part out later.

What I meant by that comparison was that Juan and I always lived a good distance away from Gummy and her husband, Poppy, but that never stopped them from visiting—all the time. In fact, since we lived so far away, they'd stay a couple weeks. And it's not like I only saw them those two weeks out of the year. Oh, no. They visited about three times a year. At least.

And once kids came, it was more...did I say one stinky dog? I meant the entire dog pound.

Let me math that for you. No matter where I ran, I mean no matter where we happened to live, I had my in-laws visiting approximately eight weeks a year. That amounts to two months. TWO MONTHS. I don't care if you live across the street from yours—do you spend that much time with them?

Know what else? They weren't satisfied with that. Not after kids came. They wanted us at their house too. If we tried to get out of it, or couldn't make it because raising a young family often means affording airline tickets isn't in the feasibility budget, they'd helpfully send us tickets.

At this point in time those visits have fallen into the good old days' realm. Poppy is gone now, and Gummy has dementia. Life is funny. Not ha-ha funny, but something smells funny, funny. Weird. Some of the most difficult moments in life can turn out to be some of the best in retrospect. Go figure.

That stinky dog may be the best dog you'll ever know.

You will miss the hell out of that dog when it's gone.

There's no doubt in my mind that I was Gummy's idea of a stinky dog, too. Only she didn't fall in love with it, her son did. After that he kept bringing it around, expecting everyone else to love it too.

Many years later when we made the life-altering decision to move to the same time zone as Gummy and Poppy, they picked out a dog for us in celebration. They claimed it was a beagle. Nobody really believed it, but before long a few family members nicknamed it The Bagel, after it broke into the garden one summer day and ate all the tomatoes.

All the tomatoes.

When I left the house that morning the dog looked like a normal low-rider dog. That evening he wobbled up the driveway with saddlebags the size of three dogs. I freaked out.

We have to call the vet!

He's going to die!

What happened?!

All the tomatoes happened.

Over the entire lifespan of that dog he never went back into any normal shape. From that day forward he wore the moniker of The Bagel. Poppy also dubbed him Waste of Fur, and Gummy shook her head and laughingly insisted he had been the pick of the litter. Beware of free dogs, she added.

The Bagel ate all the food. He bit all the neighbor kids and all the family members. Regularly. If we told him "no," he'd roll onto his back, paws in the air, and scream like he was being disemboweled. He preferred to do his business inside, on pillowcases, earning him plenty of outdoor time. On those rare occasions when he ran around like a dog, he would bark that Beagle "baroo" sound until the neighbors did threaten to disembowel him. Any time we washed him he'd find something to roll in within minutes, preferring dead minnows, worms, or roadkill.

But wow, did we miss that little shit when he died. We remember every dead minnow roll and "baroo" bark with fondness.

Did I mention life is weird? Stinky dog weird.

Two week visits from your in-laws are like that. Stinky dog weird.

At the time though, those visits akin to hanging with a stinky dog you don't much like, sucked so loudly that if you turn your ear toward the southern half of the United States, and listen carefully, you can probably still hear the echo of them.

chapter four

REMOTELY FUNNY

Weight is my Achilles heel. Sometimes I'm thin-ish—well, it's happened a couple times. Mostly I'm nowhere near, yet I'm always working on it. Even when I'm having a clandestine affair with cookies, I try my best to hide those times by tricking my fat cells with salads and the Stairmaster. Nobody is fooled, and the Stairmaster, the evil bastard of all workout equipment, is the bane of my morning workouts. Juan bought one on eBay years ago. He said it was to build up thigh strength so he could hike mountains. Sometimes we hike. Mostly we talk about when we did hike, and when we will hike at some distant time in the future. One desperate day I tried that machine because my thighs were moving into another zip code, and thus began our abusive relationship. The damn thing has been trying to kill me ever since.

The closest I ever came to really hiking a mountain was that first visit to meet the parents. Gummy and Poppy lived near a river that flowed into town from the surrounding mountains, or hills, depending on your height prejudices. Juan and another couple thought it'd be fun to go hiking. In retrospect it's obvious I was in love, because I thought that sounded like a good idea too.

We walked out the door toward the river, found the railroad tracks, and followed those until we came to a trestle. A trestle is a railroad bridge. This is where I assumed we'd turn back, and I could say, *Why, hiking is fun! We should do that again sometime!* No. I was so far out of my league.

Juan's friends had already pegged me as a bit of a princess. That's not true, although I've often aspired to it. If Juan thought I was a princess, he considered me a capable one because he had no objections when his friends and I left him in our dust. We headed into the wilds without him, since he apparently needed to spend what felt like forever staring into the river at fish. My *in love* may have covered hiking. It did not cover counting fish in a river.

Let's hike across the trestle.

You're joking. There is no railing. Why is there no railing?

Trains don't need railings. They ride on tracks.

I don't want to get run over by a train.

No trains use this anymore!

I did not want to get hit by a train while crossing a trestle, nor did I want to get arrested. Besides death and jail, the list of things I didn't want to do also consisted of walking across railroad ties where I could see rocks and the river far below. I did it, of course, because I was not going to be the unmatched-sock-wearing-wimp-princess to everyone in Juan's hometown. Halfway across Juan shouted at us from back on solid ground.

What are you guys doing?

Crossing the trestle!

Why? We're not going that way!

What? Are you serious now?

That thing's not even safe. Get off there.

In retrospect I'm pretty sure his friends were hosing with me. In the middle of the rickety bridge, I turned around and headed back, resisting the urge to crawl in relief and thankful that the path Juan wanted to take didn't involve trestles.

Yes, the path we needed to be on didn't cross the river at all. It went up and over the mountain. Did I say path? There wasn't a path. You blazed your own trail, climbing uphill while the person ahead of you let weeds and branches whip back at you. At one point we walked horizontally along a ridge, holding onto rocks, as water ran over us. In the city we call that a waterfall. In the mountains they call that runoff.

Halfway up the cliff it started to rain. This was only a problem for me, who at this point was willing to admit that *Yes, I am a princess if it will get me out of this.* One of Juan's friends suggested sitting under a nearby rock ledge until the rain stopped. Grateful, I crawled deep inside the outcropping. My clothes were wet and I had become chilly once we had stopped climbing.

You're not going to want to do that.

The wind is blowing rain inside.

You won't like it back there.

I don't care if I get dirty.

It's not the dirt. It's the rattlesnakes.

Are you effing kidding me? I decided to walk in the rain. Silently.
Rattlesnakes.
Train trestles.
Counting fish in the river.
Three things my love did not cover.
It still doesn't.

This being the last *date* I'd be having with Juan, I got a second wind, because who needs this crap? We headed up a steep incline. You had to grab onto sapling trees to hoist yourself up each step. A dead sapling came out of the ground in my hand and I slid so far down I lost one of my sneakers amongst rocks and the thick ground cover of dead leaves. Rather than go searching for it, I let it go. I kept thinking about how right now, my best friend was at Mackinac Island with her boyfriend. They were biking around the island and eating fudge. If I didn't die on this hike, I was going to go get me a boyfriend like that.

When we finally crested the top of the hill it had gotten so dark, I could barely see through the thick trees. At that point I realized we'd need to walk back down. In the dark.

Standing in the woods at the top of the mountain, wondering if there was any way I could convince Juan to go back without me and send a rescue helicopter, I noticed a man crawling through the brush. He wore a helmet with leaves stuck to it. I then realized there were several men, dressed the same, hiding on their bellies in the brush.

Uh. Juan?

Saffi, I got your shoe for you.

There are men up here!

Oh, that's just the National Guard. They come up here on
weekends to practice maneuvers.

In fact my next boyfriend would hate hiking, and rarely take me anywhere that didn't involve fudge. That's not what I said out loud. I'm not exactly sure what I said to Juan, but after I took my rescued shoe from him and whipped it at his head, he reassured me that we didn't have to hike back down. A perfectly good road lay through the forest of creepy guys in camo. The hike into town would only take an hour or two, or maybe three.

Never mind the next boyfriend. I don't care how much fudge he had; this was it for me and men. I'd go sign up for more night classes and focus on adventure and career as a single woman. Maybe I'd eventually meet guy friends who liked to dance, so I would have someone to dance with on New Year's. Maybe.

To this day I know the only reason I didn't follow through on that threat was the fortunate encounter with the driver of a pickup parked alongside that very road. He offered us a ride back to town. Of course it turned out to be a distant cousin of Juan's, because those mountain climbing, woodsy people are all related.

Back at Gummy's house she forgot about my mismatched socks, even though one got ruined due to finishing the hike without a shoe. Juan had ducked when I threw it at him and there was no locating it afterward. Once again Gummy gave Juan a little whap on the head, this time for climbing that hill with a *city* girl.

The closest I'd ever gotten to any real city was driving the beltway around, but I did my very best to look as gentrified and princessy as possible considering how cold, wet, muddy, and scratched up I'd gotten. Truthfully, I felt rather proud of having not died.

I was country too, but not as country as Juan's family, and country people can be as prejudiced as overweight people when it comes to degrees of differences. This is how experience has taught me life works. Are you from the mountains or the plains? The city or the suburbs? Do you wear a size six, twelve, or have to shop in a big girl store? People will always try to categorize you.

Gummy ran a hot bath and almost shoved me in, all the while giving Juan what for.

I liked the way she said what she thought, even if it was occasionally accompanied by her yanking off a slipper to give one of her full-grown boys a smack on the backside.

SAFFI?

I screech and almost fall off the Stairmaster. Lost in thought with my music on full blast, I hadn't noticed Gummy until she stuck her head under my arm and leaned close to shout my name. She laughs. I take my headphones off.

What, Gummy?

Never mind. I forget.

She wanders out of the room still chuckling.

Our exercise room used to be the dining room. We filled it with second-hand equipment and put Pier One room dividers in the archway in an attempt to hide everything from the neighboring front room, which has become the new dining room. I can see Gummy through the canvas flaps in the dividers. A new purse covered in glass beads sits on the table, a re-gift from one of my kids. Good thing I only give them things I want myself. A good portion of it comes back to me, on account of the fact I'm quite handicapped in the cool stuff department. Gummy examines it, turning it to and fro. Miniscule beads glisten in sunlight slanting through the windows. A brightly colored flower glitters against each black square covering the purse.

Setting it back on the table, she reaches to grab her own purse off the back of a chair. A moment later I watch as she unzips my bag and begins loading her things into it. *Okay, I guess she likes it.* To my even greater surprise, after she loads a pack of tissues and her wallet into my new purse, she adds three remote controls, one at a time, taking care to position them toward the bottom of the purse. She puts her empty old purse back on the dining room chair, pushes that under the table, and tugs my stolen purse onto her shoulder. For a moment she stands there, turning to and fro admiring it.

I get off the Stairmaster and walk into the room.

Uh, Gummy?

Saffi, look at this purse. Isn't it nice?

Yes, it is.

Someone gave it to me. I don't remember who, but I like it.

A PILE OF mismatched silverware sits in the middle of the dining room table, all that I can find. The bulk of my everyday forks and spoons have gone missing since Gummy's arrival. Gummy spends hours a day in the kitchen. My counters have never been so clean, and I can't find a dang thing I need. Today I've scrounged up mismatched plates and piecemealed a sit down dinner. It looks hodgepodge, but that's okay. Our family is all sort of like that. Random. Far from perfect. Could put more effort into looks, but will probably never take the time, because there are more important things to do. Isn't it like that for most families?

Everyone descends as food is placed on the table. Again it's a mishmash of choices. Potatoes. Salad. Asparagus. Rosemary olive oil bread and butter. Corn on the cob. Steak and fish. Most of it came directly from the supermarket, already cooked. Except the corn. That stuff is the shire's specialty in late summer. Gummy loves every bite of it. It's good to see her enjoy something. She wasn't eating well on her own. More to humor me than out of actual hunger, she puts a piece of fish on her plate. She never touches it.

Family and friends chat and laugh. Focused on her corn, Gummy doesn't say much. She looks comfortable in the crowd. I figure she comes from a large family, and she likes to be in a group. At the end of the night she gathers up dishes to carry into the kitchen and wash. I wipe down the table, and one of my kids points out something neatly wrapped in a napkin.

Mom, that's Gummy's fish.

She's pretending like she'll eat it later.

Make sure you throw that away. Who knows where she'll put it.

You're not kidding. She keeps all our remotes in her purse. We can't watch TV anymore.

Did you give her the beaded purse that I gave you? I thought you liked it.

chapter five

THE SHIRE

Since Gummy moved in with us, I've set aside my writing for a couple months to focus on her. Sometimes I get a little bit batty when I can't write. I'll type long scenes from future novels on the notes app in my phone, or on little post-it notes that I litter my office with until it looks like messy Unabomber décor.

One thing I've hung onto is that right now is the time to focus on Gummy. I thought if I took some time and devoted it to getting her diagnosed, on medicine to help with her memory, and settled here with us, then I could return to writing. Like an illogical logical person I thought that getting someone comfortable with losing their memory was a thing.

This place is beautiful.

Isn't it? I love living here.

Where are we?

The shire where Juan and I live.

What? How far is this from my house?

It takes about six hours to drive it, in good weather.

How'd you get here so fast?

We're driving to the park from my house. I packed a real picnic basket, the kind they use in movies, and a giant quilt. Gummy can't settle. She's still moving things around the house so I can't find a thing. I keep my office door shut all the time, and never go inside it in front of her. If it always looks the same, I'm hoping she doesn't notice it. Like how if you freeze when your sleepy toddler looks in your direction, they can't see you. If the things in there get stirred up, I'll never get them sorted again.

Juan drove you here the other day.

When?

Last Sunday. It was a long drive.

I don't remember that. Why'd we come up here?

So you could see the doctor.

What do I need to go see the doctor for? There's nothing wrong with me.

He already took you to see a doctor.

I can't remember the last time I saw a doctor.

You did on Monday. They gave you something to take for your memory.

What memory? My memory is crap.

They started you on memory medicine, so maybe it will get better.

Can it really? I thought there was nothing they could do.

I'm not sure how it works, Gummy. I think it can at least help it not get any worse.

You shouldn't have to do this, Saffi.

Do what?

She's eyeing me, looking very here and with it, with tears in her eyes. She motions with her hand toward me.

> This. It's not your job to take care of me. You're my daughter-in-law.

> *I'm more than that, Gummy. I'm your friend.*

She nods, and doesn't say anything more, because it's true. Also, I think she's forgotten what we were talking about.

GUMMY IS MAD at Juan. Not Juan personally, but at one of her brothers that she sometimes thinks he is. No, not really at her brother, but at her entire family because of the family secret she thinks she's uncovering.

Let me try to explain.

As if you can explain dementia.

Juan's driving and Gummy is in the passenger seat. She's chatting away and he realizes that she thinks he's her brother. The natural reaction to this situation—you know, when someone has mistaken your identity—is to correct them.

> Gummy, I'm not your brother. I'm your son.

> What?! You're my son?

> Yes, I'm your son.

> What?! Nobody told me!

> Yes. I'm telling you. I'm your son.

> Those bastards!

> What?

> All these years I've kept all their secrets! And they don't even have the decency to tell me!

> Uh, tell you what, Gummy?

About you! Nobody ever told me my big brother was my son.

This is where Juan and I differ. Odds are I'd roll right with this genetic and mathematical impossibility.

Those bastards! What secrets?

Maybe it's because I have a bit more distance. But this is Juan's mother. Being forgotten by your mother isn't just a bullet heading for the heart, it's a piece of the heart torn away and lost.

Maybe being here in the shire with us is that much harder for Gummy because she's not in her hometown with the siblings she's known all of her life. Even though we're all familiar, she often goes back in time where we don't exist. Or maybe the rational bits of her mind are trying to get back to someplace where life made a lot more sense.

EVERY SUMMER GUMMY'S family has a huge reunion at a cabin in the mountains. It's near where that plane went down on 9/11, and a beautiful woodsy area. She comes from a large family, and it took me years to sort out who was who. I'm not sure I ever really got it right. Gummy's memory problems are new; I was born with mine. Living far away and visiting her town once or twice a year didn't make it any easier to get to know her family.

It always took several cars to get our family and all the reunion supplies to that cabin in the mountains. The road in is full of deep dips, and part of the adventure is zipping over those slopes in the road and catching a bit of air as the body of the car goes up and stomachs drop. Poppy always had a couple kids in his car, and he took those rolling roads like an expert. One year, after a particularly exuberant ride over what the kids deemed 'Tickle Belly Hill,' he opened the trunk to take out Gummy's painstakingly crafted stuffed peppers. He stood there looking guilty for a moment before yelling,

"If yinz want any peppers, grab a fork and come on up here!" Everybody loved Poppy. I often wondered why Gummy didn't kill him.

Gummy's sisters cooked and baked too, and it took several picnic tables pushed end to end to hold all the food. Forever on some sort of eating restriction, I'd try to find something low in fat, low in calories, no sugar, high protein, or high fiber, whatever my diet of the moment permitted. By the end of the day, I'd usually give in and have some of everything that looked good. We'd play volleyball, where Poppy cheated shamelessly. There were games for the kids with Gummy always in the thick of it. If a relay race involved sucking down a Snicker's bar or being wrapped in toilet paper like a mummy, you could bet Gummy had a hand in it. Not only did she have a hand in it, she'd be playing too. If that meant stuffing the most balloons inside her shirt or going face first into a pile of whipped cream, no problem.

The party games for the adults weren't always very family reunion suitable.

Watching a great aunt pass the zucchini with her knees to one of the nephews home from college always seemed somewhere between inappropriate and hysterical. To raise money for next year's family reunion, they held a white elephant auction, the kind with both gag gifts and nice things. One of the uncles served as auctioneer, and Gummy always volunteered to be the one to pass out the wrapped packages to the highest bidder. She volunteered because she liked to peek at the presents. She'd count out change to the winning bidder while feeling the package with gift guessing superpowers she passed on to her grandkids. Sometimes she'd save time and tear open the end of the paper to look inside.

Gummy's siblings are a close knit group. As kids they played ball together, or Bingo, mostly willingly or sometimes because they got saddled with the younger kids. The sisters liked to tell the story about the time Gummy was being a brat and stuffed corn up her nose. This story came out of the attic at many family reunions, maybe because as the day waned on, everyone would settle down for Bingo, the game the sisters had been playing the day kid-sized Gummy took the dried corn—which was being used as Bingo chips—to cram up her nose. "For attention," the sisters insisted. All those years later, it still made Gummy laugh, and even now, long after her mother had to fish those kernels out of her nose while giving the older kids what for, I can totally see that energetic troublemaker in this seventy-something woman with dementia.

AT THE PARK in the here and now, I hop out of my Jeep and hurry around to the passenger side. Gummy stumbled getting inside. It'd never occurred to me that she'd have trouble getting in or out. Whenever we're getting into a car, I have to point out which one is mine even if it's the only car in the garage, and then I help her figure out the door handle. Every time.

Stumbling is new.

Did you hurt yourself?

I'll probably live.

Does your ankle hurt?

No.

It looks like it's getting black and blue.

It's gonna have a big bruise.

That means it's not fine.

Bruises don't mean it's hurt.

I think that's what they do mean, Gummy.

Oh, it's fine!

Usually I'll wait until she climbs in and remind her to slam the door hard. I don't know if it's all Jeep doors, but mine don't close without some serious force. It never occurred to me that I needed to spot her climbing into the Jeep. It's a bit high, and Gummy is seventy-seven now, but fit as a fiddle and as flexible as a yogi. In the morning she holds one leg up to her waist, standing on the other leg as she ties her shoe.

This is how I rate the seriousness of Gummy's injuries, if she decides to go to the doctor, it's beyond serious. Once she stepped on a piece of plate glass and cut off a chunk of her heel. She tied it back on with a bandana and continued playing baseball. About a year ago she pulled something in her shoulder and had announced she was thinking about going to the doctor for it. I asked her what happened to her shoulder and she explained she'd been doing backward somersaults with a granddaughter and yanked something.

Are you kidding me?

No. I can still do the forward ones. I guess I'm getting old because the backward ones bother my shoulder.

Are you really going to go to the doctor?

I don't know. I probably should.

If you go I want to come with you.

Why would you drive all the way here to go to the doctor with me?

Because I want to see his face when you explain how you got hurt.

Maybe she forgot about it, because she never went.

Before I reach the passenger door Gummy hops out. The door isn't shut all the way. I open it and shut it again. It's a spectacular late summer day. The land is green and blooming. The sky is crystal clear and blue. The park is in a bowl of land between low slung hills. The shire is gorgeous. If it wasn't two hours travel to get to even nowhere from this place, everyone would live here. I hurry to grab our stuff and follow Gummy as she wanders toward the pond. There's an old couple fishing there. Gummy watches them covertly and stage whispers at me.

Well, he looks like Santa Claus.

41

Gummy, how about we go sit over there?

They don't know what they're doing.

Or we could go on the other side of the pond?

Whoa, he's got a belly on him!

I practically drag her away, but she continues to narrate until they leave.

You can tell they don't know how to fish.

Maybe they're just doing it for fun.

It's more fun to catch something, but you've got to know how.

They leave and smile at us as they pass.

Poppy had a big belly but I'd never let him get that bad.

When the kids were toddlers and I had to fly, I wanted a t-shirt that said, *Sorry! Sorry!* I guess I need one for dementia too. We set up camp near the water and sit on our blanket eating egg salad sandwiches, listening to summer insects and frogs in the pond.

Aren't you afraid?

Of what?

There's no one here.

Then what's to be afraid of?

People could sneak up on us.

That's okay, I brought extra sandwiches to share.

You know what I mean. We're alone.

I can be pretty mean, Gummy. I'd beat them up and take their lunch money.

We take off our shoes and lie down on the blanket to stare at the sky. Gummy settles peacefully beside me and sings to herself. It's heavenly. When was the last time I did this? When was the last time Gummy did? I listen, thinking about the last week, and my heart aches knowing we should have checked on her more after Poppy died. None of us knew how bad her memory had gotten. We still didn't.

chapter six

SOMETHING FISHY

After the fishing trip out of Gloucester I didn't eat fish for years. Ten, to be exact. Poppy and Gummy were enthusiastic about visiting us when we lived in New England. Juan dragged a mattress into the living room of our little apartment, enthused about deep sea fishing to his father, and seemed to work late the entire visit. I spent several days rethinking our recent wedding.

Fishing isn't my thing, especially not on the Atlantic with enormous codfish reeled in and dropped to flop around the deck, seagulls circling the boat, a sea chop that almost lifted me off my feet as the boat rocked, and the guys next to me drinking something like grain alcohol out of a mason jar. In retrospect, the only fishing I enjoy is at those little roadside lobster shacks where you point out which hapless crustacean you want. That totally counts.

But I went on the boat with them *sans new husband*, because I could take time off work. Plus I owed Gummy. We weren't exactly on friendly terms after the whole wedding fiasco. Also, this involved the sea and a boat and a day off work—which sometimes sounds way better than it actually is.

A fishing village looks picturesque in photographs, but in truth it's full of dead fish, the smell of the death of dead fish, busy people, and a lot of work. It's the kind of work that wind-roughens fishermen, toughens families, and makes tourists a necessary and unwanted distraction, especially tourists who kneel in the head and revisit the last of the clam chowder they'll ever eat. Forever.

Saffi, are you ever coming out of there?

Sure. Right after the satanic clams are finished with me.

We're in a big school of fish right now. You should see.

That's exactly what I want to be doing right now. First let me see if I can die from seasickness, because, yes, yes, I think I'd rather do that than ever fish again.

Don't you feel good?

Never felt better self-disemboweling from the inside out.

I think that last bit was from the school cafeteria, third grade.

You know I feel a little queasy myself.

I hate your sitting-on-dry-land son.

You'll feel better if you let yourself throw up.

Don't put your mother's suitcase in my closet, Juan.

I have to. She packs her stuff up every night if she finds it.

When does she sleep?

Never. But she'll find it in my closet. She goes in there. Yesterday she packed all my jeans up. She thinks we're at your grandfather's cabin.

I know. I keep telling her we're not.

She can't hold onto it. Put her suitcases in the attic.

I'm tired.

Me too. I'm going to bed. You coming?

What's the point? She'll wake us up again. I'm going to
watch TV until she falls asleep.

Lately I keep my bedroom door shut all the time. I'm hoping like my
office, if Gummy never sees these rooms, she'll forget they exist. Everything in the house is in disarray. She is doing the same thing she did at her
house, sharking around in circles, moving things all day long. In retrospect,
I remember the little things we overlooked before, like her throwing away
knives with vegetable peelings, keeping a refrigerator full of expired food,
and unable to bake because she couldn't remember where in the process
she was. I wonder if we should have taken those signs a lot more seriously.
Should she have started taking memory medicine a decade ago?

Things are so much more obvious in hindsight.

It's different now. There's no question there's a problem, especially
in the evenings. Milk in the cupboard. Six cups of coffee lying around the
house. Gummy standing in front of the coffee maker or microwave trying to
figure it out with each new cup. During the early part of the day she jokes
about it.

Well, I'm losing my mind. How do you turn this microwave on?

Let me show you.

Is that all? You should have showed me before. That's easy.

In the evenings, with sundowning, everything is worse. Yesterday I
watched her walk through the house with an ear of corn from the farm stand.
She jammed it into her beaded purse. Grace is necessary.

The shire is forests, fields, and farmland. In preparation for Gummy's
arrival Juan put in an alarm system. Every time a door is opened a klaxon
blares through the house. My husband does nothing half-assed. He is metal
on metal, bone on bone, balls out, and gets stuff done.

My house is in the woods, so I think I can see why Gummy often thinks we're at the old cabin. In the mornings she watches the does with their fawns, delighted. Each day it's unexpected and new. Each day I get pulled out of the shower to look at foxes or to take a telemarketing call.

Sometimes grace isn't so easy to come by.

I thought you'd want to take that call. It sounded important.

It wasn't.

When was the last time you saw foxes up here?

Yesterday.

I fall asleep. As soon as my head hits the pillow I'm out. There are benefits to exhaustion. Juan shakes me awake.

What time is it?

Two in the morning. Gummy woke me up. She's scared. She thinks people are coming to get her.

We go to the living room to find Gummy sitting on the couch trembling, tears rolling down her cheeks. Her skin is parchment soft, folded into her pretty wrinkles, and her hands are in her lap clutching and twisting a handkerchief. She's breathing fast and loud, but trying to calm herself.

I'm sorry, Saffi. I'm sorry.

It's okay, Gummy. What's going on?

The people downstairs are coming, and they're going to get us.

Surely this fear arrived with the disease. In all the years I've known her she's been fearless. This is a woman who wielded power tools and strapped on parachutes. All her petty nerve-wracking annoyances vanish. She is genuinely terrified, and we have to help her.

I look at Juan. If we take her to the emergency room this late, it'll take them forever to check her in. She'll be even more frightened. Maybe they'll put her somewhere. Visions of a psych ward dance through my mind. Who knows if they'll even give her something to calm her down? Juan's looking at me thinking the same things. Centuries of marriage give you this mind-reading ability.

He leans close and mutters low.

Maybe some Tylenol PM?

We don't have any. Maybe Benadryl?

Juan nods and I sit next to Gummy and put my arm around her, trying to offer reassurance.

I'm not afraid. I don't care who comes. We'll keep you safe, Gummy-Gummy.

Thank you!

She's still shuddering and sobbing. I tell Juan to hurry. He's looking for those tiny plastic medicine cups. I tell him to use anything. After digging in an old First Aid Kit he manages to find Tylenol PM. He brings it and a good dose of pink liquid inside a juice cup.

Is that the kid's kind?

I don't know. Here, drink this, Gummy.

To my surprise she takes both. It looks like a lot of Benadryl. I sure hope it's the kid's stuff. Juan takes the empty cup from her and wraps a blanket around Gummy. She drops limply against the back of couch.

Oh, shit.

Oh, shit. Mom, are you okay?

She's looking around the room, light glinting off the owlish lenses of her glasses, but her eyes are barely open. She slides toward the far side of the couch, just lying there, mouth wide open, eyes now shut. *Can people die from too much Benadryl?* The look on Juan's face is pure horror. I try to sound confident.

> *I think she's okay! It's just that she went from panic attack to calm and she's exhausted.*

That feels like a lie, but I hope it's not. Oh, Lord. That was an awfully fast reaction. How the hell much Benadryl did he give her? How strong is Tylenol PM? What if it was expired? Does it get stronger?

> Let me get her into bed.
>
> *Do you think it's okay to let her sleep now?*
>
> That's why I gave it to her!

Gummy isn't very big, and I swear she's shrinking. She weighs barely a hundred pounds and looks like a child in Juan's arms. She never opens her eyes, even when we position her in her bed and take the shoes off her tiny feet.

Our bedroom is nearby. We leave all the doors open. I'm wondering if maybe I should call the emergency room when a Jurassic Park snore slithers down the hall, immediately followed by another and then another. Thank God.

We both lay there listening. I can see the headlines in my head. *Shire couple murder dementia mother-in-law with over-the-counter meds.* We live in bloodthirsty times. People like to believe the worst. Maybe they're afraid to believe the best. Either way we're going to prison. Then I play out the courtroom drama in my mind. Sometimes it's a curse to be a writer. I can see the whole thing. With dialogue.

> Do you expect us to believe this was an *accident?*
>
> *It was an emergency! We didn't realize what could happen!*

Did you suggest your husband give his mother a *glass* of Benadryl?

I just wanted her to sleep!

ASSISTED LIVING IS different than a nursing home. That's something neither of us understood. Now that we know Gummy can't go back home, Juan and I look at assisted living facilities in our area. One has an ice cream parlor, a tavern, and a classroom. It looks like a mix between an upscale college and a galleria. When they tell us the monthly cost, I laugh out loud. How can anyone afford that price? Some of the monthly rents run near ten thousand dollars.

Juan likes the posh place. Money aside, I can't imagine Gummy finding her way around there even on a good day. A smaller facility has a memory care unit, a dedicated floor with nurses and staff always on duty. Everyone has their own room and bathroom. They eat together and are entertained together. Best of all, someone is always there to offer reassurance or lead them to dinner. When they quote the monthly price of that, I can't laugh. It is a bargain seven grand a month, and that is still insane. Even if we sold all of Gummy's belongings and chipped in our own savings, it wouldn't last very long. The only other option is a nursing home. We talk about the local nursing home in her hometown. The one that smells like pee and despair. I can't do it to her, and I'm the daughter-in-law.

Gummy can't remember where she is, or when she is, but she could still shovel snow, yank the water pump out of her koi pond at home to clean it, and paint a room. She doesn't belong in a nursing home. Juan spends days going over financial records and crunching numbers, trying to figure out options.

The day I take Gummy's financial paperwork to the nearby assisted living facility to see if she qualifies for acceptance is the worst day so far. To watch the business staff crunch her numbers to see if she is worthy of acceptance wrecks me. How many people need to be in assisted living and can't afford it? What happens to them? What happens to their families and caretakers?

During those first few weeks we have to leave Gummy on occasion. One night we have a business function, and I pay seventeen dollars an hour for someone to stay with Gummy. If I paid someone so that I could work eight hours a day, it would cost over thirty-five thousand dollars a year. To have someone qualified come in is surely way out of most other people's budgets too, and forty hours a week isn't enough. Gummy needs a safe environment and qualified staff twenty-four hours a day, seven days a week, and three hundred and sixty-five days a year.

Gummy qualifies for assisted living. More importantly, this particular facility won't make one leave when they run out of money. They'll take everything she's worked for all her life, but after that is gone, they'll accept her small monthly income. We are going to do this.

Suddenly Shanghaiing Gummy out of her house to move in with us seems small. Not only have we taken her away from everything familiar, but now we are putting her into a home. The fact that we've known it could come to this makes it worse. The guilt and judgement feel blinding.

The evening after we make the deposit, I pull Gummy's suitcase out of the attic and open it. Speaking of blinding, I find inside that rancid piece of fish wrapped in a napkin. The one my kid had warned me to get rid of. I'd forgotten to throw it away at our family dinner weeks ago. Gummy had saved it for later.

chapter seven

JUST SAY NO

Dear Doctor,

My husband is heading for Singapore this week on business travel, and I'll be on my own with Gummy twenty-four-seven. I'm planning to take her to an adult day care four hours a day. They specialize in memory care.

If possible I'd like to have something to give her during a meltdown/panic attack. She's on the antidepressant you prescribed, but still has several anxiety attacks a day, and they're particularly bad at night.

She also needs a TB test and medical paperwork for her eventual move into assisted living.

Saffi, Gummy's daughter-in-law

A note to the doctor seems like the perfect solution. Otherwise I know how the conversation will go once we arrive at the doctor's office.

Hello, Gummy! How're you doing?

Oh, I can't complain. Well, I could, but who'd listen?

I'd listen, I'm the doctor.

Well, there's nothing wrong with me. I'm fine.

How's your memory?

Good! It's good! I haven't had any problems lately.

What have you been up to?

Not much. I mean we all went to the rodeo and out to dinner a couple times, but mostly I'm sitting around my house all day on my butt.

The truth is she's sharking around *my* house all day, although we did go to the rodeo and dinner, *when she visited us while we were living in Texas a hundred years ago.*

I have tried stopping in ahead of time without Gummy to explain the situation, like at the hair salon or eye doctor. It only works if I speak directly to the person who will be interacting with her. A good percentage of time that plan is met with an unhelpful, "I'll try to tell them, but you should mention it when you see them."

When I see them, I'm with Gummy and it's too late.

How does anyone think the best plan is to announce, "See this energetic lively little lady I'm with? Don't believe a word she says!" is the answer?

It stuns me that we'll fill out long medical questionnaires asking about diabetes, kidney problems, medications, et al, and not once in a four or five page medical form will it ask about dementia or Alzheimer's. None of the forms I've filled out have asked about mental health. No wonder there's a stigma—even the medical profession doesn't want to bring it up.

Meanwhile there is a person sitting behind a computer asking Gummy questions while she is mentally bopping through time and grabbing random answers out of her super nova brain.

Passing a discrete note seems the best way to go about doctor visits. As soon as we walk through the door, I hand it to the nurse and say it's for the doctor. Because Gummy will say she's fine, might be pregnant, or ask about getting a hearing aid—all things that have nothing to do with why we're there. I've seen people get side tracked or laugh at the pregnancy comment, not realizing she isn't always joking.

And there's no way in heck I'm correcting her. If she turns to me and asks for verification or help answering a question, that's fine, but normally she only does that during the memory test portion of a doctor visit. I know she is hoping that I'll give her the answers she doesn't know. Little cheater.

It backfires on her when she asks me what day it is—like I know that any better than she does. Spending all this time in Wonderland with her, I'm beginning to have trouble keeping everything together myself.

Part of the problem when interfacing with people is they can't tell she has a problem. You could sit next to her and not realize it. Sometimes she appears fine in a social setting, which is how she got so bad before we realized she needed help. I'm still learning how rough it was for her at home, and how often she was lost, or not making sense, or inappropriate, or in dangerous situations.

Keep in mind that three months before the day we mother-in-law-napped Gummy, she was living in her house, minding grandchildren, and *driving*. Driving.

I suppose hiding memory issues is normal. Most people wouldn't hide a gaping wound on their body, but if it's in their head they do.

LOOKING BACK, BOTH Juan and I have regrets. It is easier to see now what we missed. We live in a different state, and saw Gummy on holidays and weekend visits. We called often, but she's really good on the phone. We couldn't fact check her. She's a natural born B.S.er.

Right after Poppy died, I remember Gummy mentioning problems.

I'm scared.

Why? What's going on?

I think I'm losing my mind.

Gummy, Poppy just died.

At night sometimes I lie in bed and cry because I'm losing my mind.

Why do you think you're losing your mind?

I forget that I'm cooking and burn stuff.

You know I do that once a week. I've done that my whole life.

When I'm baking I forget which ingredients I've put in.

Maybe just take a break. You've gone through a lot this year. Are you sleeping?

I never sleep. You know I never sleep.

Maybe that's the problem. Did you tell the doctor?

He said I'm just getting old.

You need a new doctor, 'cause you know that's not true.

That's what I did. I tried to reassure her and joked. We must have had similar conversations before because I remember it well. What I mostly remember is that no matter how many times she might have told me, I didn't listen.

Her conversations now are a confusing mix of old facts, rearranged facts, imaginings, and a rare tidbit of truth. Just when you think nothing she says is real, you'll find out every word of a conversation was true. Or vice versa.

When we were certain she had a problem, allowing her to stay at her house as long as possible was our first priority. She must have had a lot of guardian angels and a whole lot of luck, because in hindsight by the time we thought she'd need to be out of her house soon—she should have already been.

In the early years we *had* tried to address this problem with her doctor in her hometown. I'm firmly convinced she had the worst doctor on the planet. Maybe he thought she had the worst family.

Four years before the kidnapping, when we thought Gummy was still Gummy, we took a weekend trip together. Taking her from the familiar, with new people and places in the evenings, gave us a good look at sundowning—even though we didn't understand what that was. After a very long drive during which we almost lost Gummy because she kept wandering off, we got to a hotel. We'd booked an extra room so she'd have private space to relax in, something that went without saying back then.

Now who's sleeping with me?

Nobody, but we're just across the hall from you.

But I have to sleep in that room all by myself?

Unless you want to sleep with Juan and me.

That would be weird. But isn't someone sleeping in my room with me?

Several times throughout the evening Gummy wandered across the hall to our room to ask that question. She did remember where we were, but her anxiety and the repeated questions, coupled with the getting lost at every shop, restaurant, and gas station made it obvious something had changed.

Soon after, we made the journey to her hometown. I found she'd parallel parked in a regular pull-in parking lot. Standing there with my arms crossed, I tried to figure out how on earth to get that car out. The nose rested just inches from the doors of a sedan, and the backend from another. How she got it in there should be a tribute to her mad skills in the parallel parking department.

After coming up with no ideas, I went back inside. We were at a funeral. Gummy whispered to me throughout, pointing out people and giving me incorrect backstory. I'd been married to Juan long enough to recognize these headline stories were being assigned to the wrong people.

Maybe she's grieving, I thought. She leaned close to request I ask the person in front of me if her son would be showing up. Cooperating, I did. The woman looked stricken by my question, big tears forming in her eyes.

My son died ten years ago. Today's his birthday.

Ugh! Now I remembered the tragic story and wanted to sink into the floor and vanish. I apologized profusely and made a vow to double check Gummy from then on. About ten minutes later she disappeared and I couldn't bring myself to go back to the parking lot to see how she'd gotten her car out. I still don't know. I still don't want to know.

Juan met the problem head on. At least he tried to. He convinced Gummy she'd have to quit driving and get help. At that point in time, she could be reasoned with. Why wouldn't she be reasonable? She surely saw the gaps in her abilities too. But when we involved her doctor, he said, right in front of her, that there was no reason she couldn't still drive, and that everyone has memory problems when they get older. She chose to believe the doctor. Why wouldn't she? Whenever something is wrong, who wouldn't grab onto the voice of authority reassuring us that nothing is amiss?

If I were to ever be in that situation again I would walk out of that office and go find another doctor immediately. If she'd started memory medicine then, would it have made a world of difference? We'll never know. At the time we were running our own engineering business. Most of it fell on Juan's shoulders, but I had taken on writing too, determined to get published at long last. Our kids were in college. All of us took turns driving hundreds of miles to Gummy's house to run her to doctors' appointments.

That meant back and forth from state to state. We had to get Gummy to specialists, bloodwork, scans, and an MRI. The difference in Gummy as we'd known her and her behavior at the time made us determined. Something was wrong. We were told she didn't qualify for Meals on Wheels or Home Healthcare. Other than her memory, there wasn't a thing wrong with her health. She rarely so much as took an aspirin. While looking for services that might help her we hit nothing but roadblocks. When the medical results came in and Gummy's doctor gave his diagnosis we were floored. I still remember my daughter sobbing. She knew Gummy was not okay.

In one visit the doctor had destroyed months of persuasion. We were disheartened, but it made Gummy happy, and I'm sorry to say we let it go for a time. It felt like an official notice that there was nothing we could do. We still tried to keep an eye on her, but we were also going about our own lives far away. We had no idea how much worse it would get, or how quickly.

That experience changed me. If someone says that they are having memory issues, I now believe them. There are currently no medications that will cure dementia. There is medicine that can slow it down, they think. I'll forever wish we'd gotten Gummy help sooner. I'll forever wish we'd challenged that doctor then. I'll forever wish I'd listened more closely when she first mentioned that she thought she was losing her mind.

Those opportunities for intervention with her cooperation were brief and soon gave way to faking it and deceit. I doubt Gummy is the only tricky hobbitses who can hide so many symptoms so well. I think a good litmus test to figure out how someone with dementia is really doing, is to take them out of their comfort zone, or plop yourself right into their life and stay a while. It wasn't until the kidnapping that we knew the ugly truth, and by then the window of opportunity to the best outcome had closed.

On the other hand, if we'd have tried to move Gummy out of her house any sooner, it would have taken Sauron and an army of Orcs. Sometimes I think that's what it's going to take to keep her from going back even now.

Still. I wish.

THE MEDIEVAL MANOR in Boston looked like Las Vegas's Tournament of Kings, without the jousting. It's dinner theater with audience participation, where you eat with your hands and drink grog. Juan and I took his parents. Gummy, being a staunch Methodist, doesn't drink. She jokes about drinking, but she never does it. However, when they filled our goblets, they didn't mention to her what it was.

And she drank it.

Being a loving daughter-in-law, I made sure her glass never emptied.

Back at our apartment later that night, when Gummy had figured things out and needed a bucket, she gave me what for even as Juan teased her. I've never seen anyone so stoic about throwing up. When I get sick I retreat to bed with my electric blanket, Gatorade, and books—for days if I can get away with it. Gummy barfs, and then goes about her business. I've seen her dart into the bathroom, get sick, rinse her mouth, and announce she is ready to head out for the day.

She's never been a drinker, and she's never taken medications outside an occasional course of antibiotics. The spiked punch fountain Juan and I had at our wedding shocked her a bit, especially since the minister assumed it was non-alcoholic and drank it (yeah, we got the minister tipsy too). That's not even the worst of it. The groomsmen called him an asshole during a bit of a road rage altercation. That happened the day after the wedding.

Since most of the wedding party came from other parts of the country, we started our honeymoon by taking a drive to the top of a mountain to see the view. Gummy's minister happened to be walking up the path with binoculars, bird watching. I wanted to melt into the floorboards when those guys colorfully hollered at him to get out of the middle of the road, but he took it like a man of the cloth. All I could wonder was how well my new mother-in-law would take it.

Let me back up. Gummy had had the interior of the church repainted to match my wedding colors. She thought the original paint color on the sanctuary walls would clash with the pale peach of the bridesmaid dresses. As church treasurer she managed to score paint she approved of, dig up volunteers, roll up her sleeves, and repaint the entire sanctuary.

Juan and I had taken new jobs in Boston and couldn't swing the cost of a big wedding there. Planning a wedding remotely in my hometown wasn't feasible either, but Gummy volunteered her hometown with bells on. She sent me lists of florists and bakers and venues. Somehow it all came together over the phone and via snail mail—until the weekend of the wedding, when I showed up and discovered just how helpful she'd been.

The tuxedos.

The cake.

The reception food.

The reception hall.

The wedding songs.

The church program.

The flowers.

The little doo-dads for the bridesmaids' hair.

Gummy had turned it all into her dream wedding, not going with any of my choices. I'd planned each detail, but Gummy had gone on an inspection tour and changed everything to her liking. Ascots made Poppy's neck look too big, and everyone needed to match, right? The cake needed to match the bridesmaid dresses too. She'd had reception food she liked better at a different wedding, so she contacted the caterer. The layout of the reception hall wouldn't really work because she wanted giant photos of Juan and I as babies—covered in peach crepe rosette frames—to be the centerpiece. My chosen songs had vulgar phrases like *loving you*, and *sleep with you*. Those all had to go.

In retrospect the silk garlands I'd ordered for the bridesmaids were the worst. After all these centuries I'll give Gummy that much. I made the florist change them back though, because at the time I couldn't admit it. When I saw the changes she'd made, my inner Godzilla—screw bride-zilla, I went right for destroy Tokyo in my anger mode—lost her shit as my last nerve imploded.

There's a fine line between mothers-in-law and daughters-in-law and that whole scorched earth thing.

Standing in the foyer of the reception hall Gummy pointed out that my wedding dress was entirely too low cut. It went up to my neck, but there was sheer fabric on the upper chest. With a bit of focused effort you could tell I had skin under there. After I'd changed the groomsmen tuxedos back to what

I wanted at the last minute, we discovered Poppy had gotten involved and ordered himself a tux with tails, a top hat, and a cane. We didn't mind it in the least, but Gummy sure did. She yanked his hat off his head and stomped on it just before we entered the reception hall.

We never talked about it. As far as I was concerned at the time, I'd made a huge concession by not protesting the baby pictures in ginormous peach-flowered frames. For a time following the peach wedding in the peach-painted church with the peach-colored cake, things were rather strained between us. By the time we spent enough one on one time together for me to dare bring it up, she'd long forgotten my wedding. Yes, that does mean I didn't find the courage until these last few years.

When I had my first baby and decided to breastfeed, Gummy considered me a radical over-the-top earth mother. She also seemed to think it was another chance for me to flaunt my mammaries, like with the wedding dress. If you can believe it, some generations considered breastfeeding a class distinction. My own grandmother had fourteen children. She proudly told me each of them had been fed canned milk, and that that other stuff—meaning breastfeeding—was for poor people. She couldn't even bring herself to say the word. I don't know how you can't be a poor people with fourteen kids, but every generation has their perspective and prejudices too.

Gummy and one of her relatives cornered me to insist that breastfeeding—they'd say the word, those naughty ladies—was completely unnatural. It made me laugh. I asked why feeding a human baby cow milk was natural, but all my arguments were lost on them, as theirs were on me.

In retrospect I'm certain that Gummy saved her most vehement criticisms of me for her friends and sisters, the same way I did with her. We had to try to get along whether we liked it or not. That didn't mean we had to always agree, something that took me far too long to figure out.

chapter eight

SAVE YOURSELF

Feel free to judge Juan for going to Singapore and leaving me alone with dementia. I do, although he had no choice. I understand that. Writing requires enough obsession and blind dedication that I can't judge him for an inconvenient work trip. Careers require sacrifice. Sacrifice is pain. Plus someone has to come up with the money to pay healthcare workers. We have hired one a few times so I can do something wild and fun, like get groceries, or hide in the shelves at the bookstore.

My book sales don't quite cover home healthcare workers. Coming up with the cash to pay them requires Juan's help. Thus my cooperation and support. If at any time it sounds like I'm shouldering all the Gummy stuff, notice how I'm not mentioning the mountains of red tape and paperwork she came with. A lifetime of it. Plus the house of hoarded things. Juan and I are a team. We play to our strengths.

That's one of the reasons I balked at the beginning.

I'd rather do all the things I did twice than half that effing paperwork.

Juan tells me to do whatever I have to do to survive the situation while he's gone. This ends up being Facebook posts full of TMI, a sense of humor, and letting go of all expectations—which I think I've done, but I'd forgotten about the fact that there are other people in the world. People with more time on their hands than me, apparently.

That is why with Juan in Singapore and me in the shire, I lose my shit and post the following on my Facebook:

> *It's Dude Seriously day in dementia land, and it has nothing to do with Gummy.*
>
> *She's tired today, because she was up late into the night worrying and packing. This morning I found her sprawled on the couch, fully dressed and in matching sneakers. She obliged me by enjoying yet another tomato sandwich and a ride through the country—complete with the abandoned Pitbull I tried to rescue and shove into the time travel jeep—to adult day club.*
>
> *My Dude Seriously is because rumors in her home-town have crossed state lines.*
>
> *I probably shouldn't address them, but Dude Seriously, I'm going to.*
>
> *Dear Haters and Gossipers,*
>
> *Subject: Me Selling Gummy's House and Purchasing a Yacht to Sail the South of France and Live Off the Proceeds*
>
> *The rumor is entirely true.*
>
> *SO SUCK IT. MWAHAHAHAHAHAHA.*
>
> *Yes. I married Gummy's son and hung on for eighty billion years so I COULD DO JUST THIS.*
>
> *HAH!*
>
> *Yes. Working all these years WAS A FRONT.*
>
> *Hell, investing every cent from the working in order to found a startup engineering business was also a FRONT.*

All those engineering conferences I wanted to jam picks into my ears during was ALL JUST A FAKE OUT!

BABIES. LATE HOURS. BEING DRAGGED AROUND THE COUNTRY. ROOM MOTHER. RAISING BUTTERFLIES. IT'S ALL JUST SMOKE AND MIRRORS, BABY!

The night owl writing and the books I've written and published and sold? Just part of the trickery. HAH YOU ALL BOUGHT IT DIDN'T YOU?

I admit the whole damn thing. It was all with my eye on waiting for the right moment to sell Gummy's house and WALLOW IN THE BANK. Everyone knows that three bedroom one bath 1,200 SQFT fifty-year-old homes in defunct factory towns ARE SOLID GOLD, bitches.

I'm going yacht shopping.

SEE YOU LATER SUCKERS!!!!!!!!!!!

If you missed it, at this point I've spent weeks unable to sleep, shower or exercise without one ear listening for the *klaxon alarm* of our security system alerting me to Gummy attempting to escape. My days are spent answering the same questions on repeat, and trying to help her understand where she is and why. At this point I've become convinced that dementia must be contagious, because when you spend your days in Wonderland, you become fluent in the language of nonsense, and reality begins to drift.

Yet back in her hometown, there's a rumor that I've taken my mother-in-law for her money. If I ever have time to balance my checking account, I can dispel that myth fairly quickly.

IT IS FOGGY this morning in the shire, and the tops of the hills look like islands surrounded by a sea of clouds. Gummy loves when the jeep breaks through the clouds into full on sunshine. She's full of compliments for this place. She loves the hills, woods, streams, and how clean everything is. Of course she doesn't want to live here. She thinks to add that sometimes. She has her own town, and she wants very much to get her memory better and go there.

I don't tell her about the terrible flood in her town yesterday. The last thing she needs is one more thing to worry about. She's not a worrier by nature. She's a worrier by necessity. Home or here, she's now forever in a strange place and doesn't know what's going on. Her natural instinct is caution and worry.

When we drive or walk, sometimes she feels safe and she'll take a break from her chronic worrying and talk.

Sometimes she tells me about what it was like to be the ninth child of eleven, or how Dahlias remind her of her mother. Today she gave me a glimpse into her present.

> Talking is hard. So many people have died, or gotten old, or grown up. I've known a lot of people. Sometimes I mix them up. I'm old. I have to think of the right people, and know if they died, or something. When I talk they say, no, I'm not him, or I'm not in Texas. Then I forget what I was going to say, and have to think all over again.

It is astonishing how often dementia reminds me of the way children sometimes are. Once my daughter was talking so fast I couldn't follow—the words gibbered together. I crouched down to her level and said, "Hold on, I can't understand you. You're going too fast." My little girl huffed, "MOM, I don't care! I'm talking right now!"

Maybe that's it. I think I get that. Sometimes talking is thinking out loud. Sometimes it's just a need—LISTEN TO ME. Maybe we don't have to always understand the words. I know some monks who have a saying, "Listen, it is the best gift you can give." So I'm listening, and wow is it tiring—but even when the words don't make sense, I hear her.

OVER THE YEARS when the in-laws inflicted their two-week visits on us, Juan didn't always have to work. I don't want to exaggerate that fact against him. Sometimes he did secure time off so he could take his father fishing or hunting, and leave Gummy and I to spend quality time with each other or the kids.

I never thought about leaving him over the parental visits. Occasionally I thought about killing him though.

One day he came back from a *bird hunt* in Texas. Birds. Yes, sweet, innocent birds. Not only had he gone off to murder angel birds, but he returned with his dog covered in oil. Apparently Gunner Boom, a bird dog himself and very self-satisfied with his day of hunting, had gotten hot. This being Texas, he'd had the misfortune of trying to cool off in a puddle full of oil instead of water.

Head to toe tar puppy.

I took one look at that beautiful, clever dog dripping with thick, sticky tar and announced we obviously would need to get a new dog.

I loved that dog, but not that much.

My love is finite. I'm sorry, but I'm a realist here. I might die for a dog, but I'm not cleaning tar out of his orifices. I might have grown to love Gummy, but I'm not cleaning the basement she's been hoarding shit in for an entire lifetime.

All the crap I threw out whenever I moved state to state that Gummy nabbed to "give away" is in that basement. The interesting things she spotted tossed to the curb by people over decades are in that freaking basement. Rummage sales. Clearance sales. Thrift stores. All of it is in that basement.

Once during a visit, she asked Juan and me to move an ancient, heavy-as-a-black-hole air hockey table to the other room of her enormous basement. He agreed. Juan is an extremely helpful and good guy. I know this, although I forget it when he leaves his mother with me when he goes to Singapore, or when he gets on my nerves, or during fishing or hunting season. But other than that.

I love you, I said as we hoisted that table and our spines creaked dangerously.

I love you too, he said.

No. I really, really, love you.

I really, really love you too!

I want you to know that. How much I love you. And know that if anything ever happens to your mom, it's still not enough love for me to EVER clean this basement.

I stand by that.

Gummy would never be like that. She's better than me at everything. After one glance at that oily dog, during which I dismissed him entirely, she took a bottle of Tide, grabbed him by the collar, and hauled him into the backyard where she proceeded to wash him. Forever. Given the amount of time it took, I'm surprised it's not one of her stronger memories.

It wasn't long enough.

The dog didn't come clean, but it made enough of an impact that I thought perhaps Gunner Boom could be recycled with professional help. At that point he just looked like one of those sad birds from an oil spill, but I paid the vet all of our money to turn him white and orange again.

Whatever they did to him, it made him speak in tongues anytime I tried to take him to the vet ever again.

WHEN THE KIDS went down for naps, Gummy and I would paint. Sitting at the glass table in the kitchen of my first house, the one that would someday get flattened by a tornado after we'd again moved away, we would slip into creative mode together. The Texas sun brightened the room with such enthusiasm we couldn't help but go with it.

The guys weren't on a bird or fish murdering spree that time. They were better employed doing yardwork in our postage stamp size, fire-ant infested yard. Gummy and I were making baskets covered in silk flowers. With enough paint, glue, and some sort of sealing spray Gummy knew about, the finished project looked like a ceramic bowl. Gummy is a professional painter. Some of her work used to be sold in local shops around her hometown.

All of her silk flowers were painstakingly painted using several colors, with highlights and lowlights. Mine were painted on the front only, and glued onto the basket with bare backs.

What are you doing?

Finishing this in this lifetime.

Why aren't you painting the backs of those flowers?

Because they're glued to the basket and you can't see the backs anyway.

That's the wrong way to do it.

Why? No one can see it. It doesn't matter.

Well. It matters to me.

One of the windows exploded inward, showering us with glass and blowing shards the entire length of the kitchen and out the doorway on the far end. We looked at each other.

What the hell was that?

I don't know.

I think someone is shooting at us.

I think you might be right.

We both moved closer to the window and looked outside to see if we could spot the culprit.

Why would someone be shooting at us?

I don't know. This is Texas.

I don't see anyone.

That window definitely looks like a bullet hole came through. See the hole? Only the second pane exploded.

Oh! We probably should duck or something.

Oh, yeah…

We laughed and laughed, and if it had been an assassin that's the part where we would have died. Fortunately it was just Poppy outside, dragging the lawnmower over gravel.

My fake ceramic basket didn't survive the move out of that house, but the memory of that day is one we've laughed at over the years. I doubt Gummy remembers it now, but I tell her those stories sometimes. I tell her how Juan always had to work, and how much I hated fishing, how she'd doused the hapless dog with Tide, and we tried to spot the assassin rather than duck for cover. She laughs, and that connection we forged over the years, the one made of odds and ends like dryer lint, hot glue, and shards of glass, reappears, if only for a moment.

Her recall for why we're so often together now has been destroyed in whatever slow deterioration is taking place in her head. But I'm sure that somewhere in Gummy's basement of hoarder's dreams that old silk flower covered basket still sits, withstanding time better than brain synapses. Yet, I swear to God. I am not cleaning that basement.

chapter nine

I SEE DEAD PEOPLE

Juan worries that he's not patient enough with Gummy.

He's back. She never noticed he'd gone.

As I've said I think it's easier for me.

As a writer I thrive on non-linear, abstract thought. Suspending rationality is my idea of a good time.

But, good lord, to an extent!

Little Ferrety-McFerret, in addition to carting around all our remotes in her purse, has now gone a step further.

We're driving and she's rooting through her purse as usual. She needs to have her wallet with a few dollars and her debit card or she cannot relax. If she doesn't have her purse she'll spend all of music therapy class and adult day club hunting for it in a state of near panic.

She also *must* have her glasses, either in her purse or on her nose. This is a bone of contention because she had cataract surgery and doesn't need them anymore. Since she's always worn them though, that's how it has to be. I thought she was seeing dead people and things that weren't there—but I'm pretty sure, hopeful I should say, that most of the time she is just looking at life through double her prescription.

The day before we brought Gummy here, I took her to the cemetery to put flowers on Poppy's grave. It's one of those cemeteries with flat head-stones. *The better to mow over you, my dear.* Poppy's grave is at the crest of a rolling green hill, and every time we go there, we can never find it without walking a good portion of that hill. Cicadas were doing their frenetic thing, and shimmering heat waves billowed off the crisscrossing roads between patches of markers as we searched.

Despite the heat, Gummy marched from marker to marker, looking for Poppy's grave. When we found it, we sat to pull weeds off the edges of his headstone. Gummy placed a new artificial arrangement in the perfect spot among faded others.

Look at all the people here.

I look around and see no one. It's crickets. Or cicadas.

I've never seen so many people in this place!

I look behind me. Nope. It's all low-slung hills and headstones. Not a soul in sight.

Just look at them all! What's going on? See that woman right there? She's looking at us.

Gummy points. I push her hand back down. I don't believe in ghosts, but neither do I point at the ones who are looking directly at me.

I will have the lenses replaced with plain glass or a new prescription soon, so she can quit freaking me out.

Today she's bouncing along in the passenger seat of my Jeep, rooting through her bag and I hear the telltale jingle of car keys. One set, and then another set, like if you're here in the shire and missing your gol-dern keys, let me know. There's a good chance little Ferrety-McFerret has them where she stores the rest of her pirate booty.

The worst part is, usually in the morning when she's at her best, she'll get in there and say—why on earth is this in my purse? Except those remotes.

She checks to make sure they're there with her wallet and debit card. I wonder if she thinks it's her cell phone. No good can come of asking too much and risking embarrassing her.

I don't like watching TV anyway.

Gummy didn't notice Juan had gone because she can't remember where she is or who should be here. I'm becoming her human equivalent of a seeing-eye dog. I try to tie her down with stories of where we've been and what we've done. Juan is mine for the logical world. I sure noticed he'd gone. The color logical tends to elude me. When he gets home, all travel-weary and suffering from jet lag, I kiss him hard, shove Gummy and a pile of paperwork into his lap, and escape into the world of story before all this reality can crush my soul.

GUMMY FOLLOWED HER father-in-law across the grass.

Do you remember where they were buried?

Yes! Right over that hill. I remember. Back then they took coffins to the cemetery with a horse and buggy.

Everyone called Gummy's father-in-law Pappy. Inside the old cemetery he led us around tombstones so old I couldn't read what they said anymore. They were the kind that stood taller than we did, which isn't saying much considering Pappy and Gummy's height. I followed them, doubting Pappy really remembered where his grandparents were buried, but this was better than spending the day with the rest of the guys. They'd taken off to go rabbit hunting, and hunting is not my thing. Although earlier in the relationship I had been stupid in love enough to try. *Part-time vegetarian goes hunting and other lovesick conundrums.* I spent that day bellowing out "There's one!" to purposely scare rabbits off. I'd been dead to the guys and their sportsmen pursuits ever since. That's what I consider a win.

In an effort to find something to do with her daughter-in-law, Gummy had taken me to visit her in-laws. They lived near her and really couldn't believe that I'd give up a day of rabbit hunting. I peppered them with questions about family history. Knowing my penchant for old cemeteries, Gummy suggested this trip. Pappy complied because she sweetened the deal with the promise of ice cream.

According to Pappy we found family gravestones, although the spelling of the last name had changed so much Gummy and I weren't so sure. The top of one of the ornate markers had fallen off. We debated what should be done about it. Standing in blistering heat in a cemetery with my mother-in-law and Juan's grandfather, with the top of a grave marker in my hands, I was oddly and perfectly happy. I don't know what it is about cemeteries. I like to haunt them. I keep a collection of names I find on headstones. I think that it is the potential of all those stories that lures me. I was the only one having a good time. Pappy just wanted his ice cream. Gummy just wanted to humor her weird new daughter-in-law.

It's painfully ironic how much family time ends up taking place around cemeteries. Maybe Gummy and I are some of the only ones that had pleasant times in them. Once she knew I liked going to them, whenever she got bored with me during a visit she'd drag me off to look at another one—pointing out distant family while I jotted down names for my collection.

We stopped going not long after I had kids. Once you have to drag one of your kids out of an open grave, it loses its appeal, even for me. One summer day we searched a mountaintop cemetery for Gummy's mother's marker. We spent more time hauling my toddler off or out of freshly dug holes, where she'd sprawl face down and wallow like some sort of Flounder on the sea floor. We finally gave up on finding it and focused on cleaning dirt out of all that kid's face holes. That was the last time Gummy and I went to a cemetery together. Until we had to.

AS SOON AS I lifted the phone from the cradle and saw the name on caller ID, I knew. After eons of marriage, this was this first time anyone in Gummy and Poppy's family had called me. I knew someone had died.

My kids were summoned from school, an emergency suit purchased for the oldest, luggage packed, and miles raced over. We met up with Gummy at the funeral home in her hometown. Grief shrinks people. Standing in the coffin room, she looked like a child with an aged face and a broken heart. Her left arm, the one the obstetrician had to dislocate when she'd been born in order to tug her tiny body from her even tinier mother, had suffered permanent nerve damage. She can never raise it very high, and always holds it at an awkward angle, sometimes using her other hand to force it into position. Today it clutched a plastic baggie with Poppy's personal effects: a wallet stuffed with the secrets of the universe—all the keys, coins, Rolaids, and his watch.

A coffin salesman touted the longevity and security of various coffins for a body now in need of neither. Not bothering to pretend to listen, we melded together to hear the family story of *how*. What Happened? Having told it several times, Gummy spoke in that empty rote voice of someone who isn't really there. We listened with unwilling desperation clogging our hearing. It had taken nearly a day to get there, and the *to do* list was long.

Should we get an autopsy?

How many days will this take?

What should he wear?

Where will we put him?

Who is in charge here?

Go away, go away, go away.

None of it mattered to Gummy, and she answered in the same uninhabited voice, requiring only nods of approval from everyone. We cooperated and nodded some more, even when she requested a three day viewing so everyone could come.

Three days? Juan? Three days?

Shhh.

Since I've never lived anywhere long enough to put down deep roots, I didn't know what it looked like to pass away in a small town where you'd lived a very long life. Flags flew at half-staff along the main street. The entire town filed through the funeral home, hour after hour, day after day. Flowers fought for space. Family fought for footing. Fried chicken fought for room in coolers and refrigerators as trunk load after trunk load of food arrived.

Brothers argued over suits.

Relatives argued over rumors.

Lovers argued over old lovers.

Everyone came for three days.

Seated on a low chair near the protective coffin, Gummy greeted each and every person. She'd inspected all the flowers, directed the footing of each family member in need of help, sorted suits and clothing like a mom overseeing funeral fashion, and found a place for each piece of never-ending fried chicken. She soothed hurt feelings caused by ugly rumors, pointed out which people she didn't want at her funeral, and made me repeat all the details of the quarrels she'd missed. Those little bits of gossipy gold are excellent distractions from the blinding suffering of great loss.

A few years later, Gummy promptly forgot it all.

GUMMY'S FAVORITE PART of adult day club might be the drive. The arrival is always a surprise. She never remembers it. Each and every day we get there, she wonders out loud where this place is and what's going on.

This is a nice place.

It is.

Look at those flowers.

I hop out of the Jeep and race around it, hoping to get to her before she tries to get out by herself. Sometimes she beats me to it. Sometimes she looks at me blankly when I open the passenger door.

Am I getting out here?

Yes.

Oh, I didn't know that. Should I bring my purse?

Yes.

This is really nice. Look at those red flowers. I don't remember what they're called.

Flowers.

Smarty pants.

But she laughs.

You don't remember any better than I do.

You might be right about that.

We walk past all the signs announcing the assisted living facility and adult day club. She doesn't notice them, but comments on the coffee urn in the lobby. Every morning.

That smells good.

I'll get you coffee in that room downstairs.

That would be good. I'd like a cup of coffee.

I think they have zucchini bread today to go with the coffee.

That sounds even better.

The staff in day club is amazing. As soon as Gummy walks in and asks what this place is, they swarm her, getting her a cup of coffee and ushering her to a seat. She gives me the evil eye.

Where are you dumping me?

The workers interrupt to ask if there's any chance she can hang around here for a little bit and help them out today.

Oh, I could probably do that.

Gummy has only attended for a couple weeks, and the staff already knows how best to include Gummy and ensure her cooperation. She's spent a lifetime volunteering, and is more than willing to help them out with all these old people.

When I pick her up four hours later, she's anxious to go. Sometimes she tells me it was boring and that she doesn't know why she goes there, but she's not a big complainer so even on those days she'll admit it wasn't bad. But no matter her mood she's happy to see me and forgets where she's been by the time we exit the parking lot.

UGH.

Tonight is full-on hallucination night.

Not nearly as much fun as it sounds.

Gummy isn't eating because she's absolutely positive she already ate with a bunch of family members that have been dead and gone for at least a decade.

And she ate so much with them she's stuffed full.

She thoughtfully wrapped up our leftovers from the food she wouldn't touch. Placing them in kitchen garbage bags she put them into the fridge. Except the spaghetti. That went into her purse.

Dear Hubby found her in my closet looking for pants.

Kind of ironic because she weighs about as much as a fourth grader.

I'm at least eighth-grader sized. STFU.

She wears size ten pants because "I always wear a ten." Yeah, she's about a size two. She looks like someone put Lowly Worm into Hilda Hippo's pants.

Pretty sure these meringue cookies I'm eating as I write will make everything better. STFU.

I DON'T WANT to know.

I don't want to know how bad this is going to get.

Don't get me wrong, I use Google like an addict. I shop with it and check reviews and research most everything. With writing research is imperative. I also fact check in person whenever possible. I've hopped out of an airplane in order to know how terminal velocity felt. Once I ate insects for a story. Chocolate *chirp* cookies are pretty good. I prefer to eat vegetarian, but I'll try the unnamed meat in a fishing port somewhere in Greece, because these details are necessary to me. I'll hike to the bottom of the Grand Canyon, or ride the open cockpit plane. And I'll usually go to the places I write about. I want to know what it smells, sounds, and tastes like.

Research is my bag.

Minutiae and particulars are critical.

Still, there are things in life I prefer not to know everything about. It's a choice. Parenthood. Starting your own business. Trying to get a book published. Stage six dementia.

I don't want to know.

I do enough research so that I understand the skeletal structure. After that I don't want to know how much pain is involved. I'll find out soon enough. Walking blindly into a shit storm is probably no worse than walking in with your eyes wide open. I think it buys me a few more minutes of whistling in the dark.

If I have a philosophy, it's that I will never know the end of the world is coming until it's too late. I don't see the downside.

chapter ten

THE SMELL OF DESPAIR

Gummy has moved into assisted living.

The memory care unit.

She has a tiny apartment, and when she steps into the hallway she's greeted by aides or nurses. They reassure, redirect, calm, sympathize, assist, offer snacks or give her medicine. They take her to activities and meals, and stand shoulder to shoulder like linebackers when she packs her stuff and makes a run for the exit, insisting she's leaving.

After all this, they unpack her stuff, dig her remotes out of her purse, throw away the food she's hidden in napkins, and all the other stuff we did at home with her.

They have a team that only has to pull eight hour shifts.

Thank God.

IT'S LITTLE DETAILS I always remember best. Gummy letting my kids eat Cheetos on her good couch, the white one with big peach colored flowers. She taught them to use a fork so their fingers wouldn't turn orange. Gummy bought that couch to go with the peach colored carpet that she'd laid in her house when Juan and I got married. My best friend got married a few weeks before I did, and picked the colors I liked, so I ended up saddled with peach, without ever caring for it at all. After all these years, I consider it Gummy's décor color.

Despite the peach and Poppy's penchant for camo or fishing gear cluttering up corners of the house, Gummy always made her home beautiful.

Maybe she doesn't like peach either. Wouldn't that be ironic?

If Gummy needed new tile in her bathroom or kitchen, she usually put it down herself. She painted ceilings and walls, put up shelving, and artfully arranged handfuls of *things* until it resembled something out of a magazine. When people complimented her work, she'd modestly wave it away.

> That's just a bunch of junk I found.

> It really needs a bit more greenery around the edges, don't you think?

> That old thing? You really like it? You can have it.

Outside she worked her yard into a little bit of Shangri-La with a koi pond and waterfall. Digging, planting, ripping apart pumps and cutting down tree limbs, she even managed most of the heavy lifting herself. Her yard likely holds bits and pieces from everywhere we lived or visited. If Gummy saw a plant or flower she liked, she'd dig that thing up, wrap it in wet newspaper, and take it home to plant. Everything always grew, and Gummy filled her yard with apple trees, clover for the kids to play in, and other plants and flowers that are beyond my capability to identify, let alone keep alive. The fish were likely purchased, but the frogs possibly kidnapped from a wayside pond somewhere.

It wasn't only the spaces in her home she tried to make beautiful. She'd point out the cobwebs in my house.

> Don't you ever sweep your ceilings?

> *Is that really a thing?*

> That would drive me crazy.

I never look up there.

It's making me nuts.

Feel free to sweep my ceilings. I want you to be comfortable here.

Thanks a lot.

She'd do it though. She'd also enthuse over any bit of domesticity I'd haphazardly toss into my life.

Are those new drapes?

Yes!

They look great. Where'd you get them?

Someplace at the mall. They were going out of business and I got them on clearance.

I can't believe how well they fit your windows. Those are odd-sized windows.

They didn't fit. I had to hem them.

You hemmed drapes?

Yes. Well. I made them fit.

Shooting me a suspicious look, she went to inspect them and discovered my secret. I'd ironed the hem in and used packing tape to hold it into place.

You're kidding.

You're not supposed to look!

That looks ridiculous.

You said they looked good.

Well, they do until you turn them around.

Only you do that.

During holiday visits, which were her specialty, Gummy would arrive with Easter or Christmas in a suitcase, and decorate the house and yard, or entertain kids with some new treasure, like a musical toy or jars of paint. Sometimes we'd holiday shop together. I remember her buying my son the car of his dreams when we couldn't afford it—a kid's Coupe Car.

On a visit to Texas, she brought boxes of ceramics and taught my kids how to paint them. On my kitchen table, dammit. The table she found at a secondhand store and helped refinish.

For years she came at New Year's so Juan and I could go out, and she let the kids stay up late and do all those things grandparents allow that parents don't.

Once when she made her famous orange cookies, she let the kids use toy backhoes to *help*. There was flour everywhere.

I have another crystal clear memory of us attending a preschool concert and Gummy laughing so hard at *Away in the Manger* sung with Texas accents that she had to duck down in the church pew to stifle it.

Haid. They said lay down his sweet haid.

The way she always played also sticks in my mind. The bouncy castle, trampoline, paintball, neon markers, fruit roll ups, sledding, and juice boxes. Gummy always participated right alongside the kids.

One time she spilled Sprite all over the table in a restaurant, and laughingly blamed it on my preschoolers. I thought they were going to beat her up.

When Juan needed more orthopedic surgery (because when you live life balls out, you need a lot of it), Gummy would hop a plane and come watch the kids to help out. When I had lengthy hospital stays during my problematic second pregnancy, there she'd be, painting a room, letting my son eat at McDonald's, and commenting I looked like hell and to hurry up and pop that baby out by Tuesday because she had a flight to catch.

When Gummy and Poppy sold their little corner grocery store they'd run for ages, Gummy took a job managing a Burger King. Poppy didn't like it.

That's a job for teenagers.

I like teenagers.

It's beneath you.

What are you talking about? I want extra money to pay for airplane tickets to go see my grandkids whenever I want.

Those memories clog my heart as I shop for furniture to put in her room at assisted living. A pretty white wrought iron bed with a mattress like a cloud, and Target's best bedding, and bedside tables. A couch with a pretty floral print. Scented drawer liners. Bath and Body Works plug-ins, soaps, and lotions. Pillows, an entire cart of full-price pillows, covered in lace and crochet.

Guilt gifts.

While Juan fills out paperwork in the business office and Gummy plays Bingo downstairs in the day club, I drag her things up the service elevator into her new room and arrange them just so. Pictures, paintings, knick-knacks from her house. I walk into her private bathroom with a load of fluffy towels and burst into tears.

It smells like pee.

There is no way. I call Juan, crying.

She'll have a meltdown, I say. Of course it won't be as big as the one I'm having, but I am not leaving my mother-in-law anywhere that smells like pee. Housekeeping comes. Maintenance comes. I plug in four of those scented oil room fresheners and hide containers of scented beads up high, hopefully out of Gummy's reach. The coordinator from the business office stops by takes one look at me and marches me down the hall to look at other available rooms.

Fifteen minutes before Gummy is due to come upstairs, I pick a new room overlooking the gazebo in the garden below. Maintenance begins moving everything, right down to the scented drawer liners, and I go downstairs, find Gummy, and take her for another ride.

WE GO TO the park, walk around the pond, and lie in the grass watching the airplanes and clouds. I talk nonsense, saying anything to distract both of us. We play with my phone, taking pictures, fooling with Snapchat, and FaceTiming Gummy's grandkids.

After hours in day club Gummy wants to rest. Hanging out in the park with me isn't what she wants to do. She wants to go home, not my house, but home. I take her to Burger King and buy her a large soda before returning to assisted living.

Juan is sitting on the couch in her new room when we walk in.

> What are you doing here?
>
> Waiting for you.
>
> Why?
>
> Do you like this place?

Gummy looks around the room and answers politely. I'm certain she'd have answered the same no matter what she thought.

> It's nice. This place is very nice.
>
> Would you be okay staying here?
>
> Why would I stay here?
>
> If you stay here, we can get you to the doctor who can try to help with your memory.
>
> How long would I have to stay?
>
> I don't know for sure, Mom. Your memory would have to get better to go home.
>
> Well, I can't stay long. I have to get back home to my kids.
>
> Do you want to get help for your memory?

Yes. I'll stay with you if you think it might help.

The problem is that sometimes we can't be there with you. I have to be at work all day, and Saffi has writing things.

That's okay. I can go home.

You can't go home, because you can't be alone. Someone has to be with you.

I could go stay with my big sister then.

Juan and I exchange a quick look. Gummy's big sister died years ago.

You would need to stay here.

But not all the time. You can come and go as you want to. Juan and I live only ten minutes from here.

Do you really?

Yes, and so do the kids. They live even closer.

Really? Nobody told me that.

Mom, are you okay staying here for a while?

I could stay here for a couple weeks, if it'll help.

That particular exchange goes easier than we could have imagined. If we'd ever dared let ourselves imagine it. What we don't realize then is that we will never finish putting Gummy into assisted living. We don't realize that process will never end.

SOME DAYS GUMMY waits for Poppy.

Where is he?

Poppy is coming to get me, isn't he?

Did something happen to Poppy? Did he leave?

Don't tell me he died.

Most days I try to pull amusing anecdotes out of my bag of tricks, trying to distract a grown woman like a toddler.

> *Hey, Gummy. Do you want to go get ice cream?*
>
> *Let's go do a puzzle.*
>
> *Do you want to go for a walk? The sun is shining.*
>
> *I brought mail! You have a letter! It's sealed with a kiss—*
>
> *or spit. One of those.*
>
> *Guess what I brought? Magic markers! Let's go make a mess!*

Sometimes it works. Sometimes it doesn't.

Looking into the eyes of my mother-in-law when she asks if Poppy is alive, I try to lie big. Mostly I can't. She knows even if I'm too big of a wussy to say it. Like the song says, *You can't hide your lying eyes.* When I watch hers and tell the truth, I can see her heart splinter.

Imagination is infinite, and so is pain.

chapter eleven

HAVE IT YOUR WAY

In assisted living Gummy can come and go as she pleases, but not by herself.

We can visit her there anytime, and bring her home with us anytime.

She can still go to day club. She can get her hair done, or her nails, without leaving the building.

She can go to the library, exercise, do crafts, get ice cream, or play games with her new friends.

Despite all the bells and whistles, we knew it would be a big adjustment that would take some time.

We didn't know every day would be a big adjustment. Or that every day the big adjustment would be almost brand new.

And we didn't realize Gummy wasn't the only one who needed to adjust.

She lives there, but she isn't often there. Not really. Not mentally. She's visiting me in Texas, where I haven't lived in many years, or she's back at her house where she used to babysit grandchildren, or she's at the family cabin, or she's thinking about moving in with family members long since passed.

Today she calls as soon as I roll out of bed, because she has a phone in her room and an entire staff and switchboard to help if she has trouble calling.

I'm calling from Burger King. Is this the place I call to let you know this will be my last day?

Uh, yes.

Oh, thank God. I quit. I quit this place. I've been through hell.

Okay.

I'm glad I figured out who to call. Thank you.

I hang up the phone and think *now that's weird.* Instinctively I know what she wants. It's like if a friend texts the word CHOCOLATE, I know she needs an emergency escape from a bad day. If Juan asks if I want to go to a movie, that always means he needs a distraction, or he thinks I do.

GUMMY THINKS THE aides and nurses in her memory care unit are coworkers from when she worked at Burger King. They're good with humoring her, or trying to distract her. The problem is she thinks she runs the joint. When they won't give her a ride home she gets really pissed at them, especially when she offers to let them count the time they drive her as paid time.

I'm your boss and I need a ride home. Why are you being so difficult?

It's not like they can tell her the truth. She can't handle the truth. It'd be like someone you work with plopping down next to you and explaining how you don't really work here, but you're somewhere getting your memory treated, and everyone is actually there to take care of you.

It might not even freak you out, because likely you'd just think they'd lost their minds.

It seems to me that her memory is compartmentalized. It's like there are gaping holes in it that are occasionally bridged. Some days she remembers Poppy died, if only for a moment. When she forgets who someone is, that doesn't seem to mean it's permanently deleted. If we can get her centered, focused, and calm, things might come back, at least for a time.

It just never stays.

Right now Gummy is sitting by the front door in the dementia unit waiting for her ride home, because those uncooperative employees of hers aren't helping.

Later she'll stage whisper to me that she's thinking about firing them.

Sitting and waiting is good, because about an hour ago she was rushing the nurses trying to get out.

They called me to call her and try to talk her down. She was behaving like an *angry escape risk*, and sick to death of Burger King, and going to walk home.

So I did what daughters-in-law have done to mothers-in-law for centuries. I threw her son under the bus.

> *When Juan gets out of work, I'll tell him you want him*
> *to come over.*

Tell him I need a ride home from Burger King.

Sure thing, Gummy.

When I call later, she is still waiting, but fortunately for Juan has forgotten for whom, because she now claims she's been trying to call that man she used to be married to. She explains she hasn't seen him in some time.

Dementia is the saddest story you'll ever laugh at. This time Gummy's stomach hurt. Her stomach has been hurting since she started the memory medicine. The doctor prescribed something for that, too. That's how drugs work, right? Medicine for the problem. Medicine for the medicine.

I tell her that she'll get her new stomach medicine in the morning.

From the Burger King nurses?

Yes, from the Burger King nurses.

You might want to buy Burger King stock because they're apparently making some serious innovations into customer service.

Seems I'm becoming quite a proficient big fat liar. Ah, well. I can't handle the truth either.

GUMMY IS YOUNG, fit, and strong. She has the strength and flexibility of a woman decades younger, because she's always been an active person.

Other than her memory and those misfiring data processing units in the brain, she's perfectly healthy.

She is not ready for a nursing home.

So, thank God. Thank God someone thought of alternative options to help care for people in situations like this.

Because some days, sundowning requires an entire staff.

Sundowning?

It's a dementia or Alzheimer's term. It means later in the day, as the sun goes down, a person with memory problems will get far far worse. I've discovered it means they have no idea where they are, why, or what the heck is going on.

It's not just Gummy. I see others with memory loss do it too.

Today a woman came barreling out of her room, furiously angry. It made me realize how lucky we are. Gummy is good-natured. When she gets angry, there's almost always good reason. So far anyway. Let's not think too hard on that one.

Since I was the only one in the hall at that moment, the woman came after me.

WHY DID YOU SAY I SMELL?!

Oh. I would never say that about you. You don't smell at all.

Someone said it!

That's rude!

It is!

She looks around for someone else to blame. Gummy is meandering up the hall behind me.

> Who said I smell?!

> I don't know.

Gummy leans in and sniffs her.

> But you don't.

She continues glaring for a moment, then sags.

> I'm just going to go back to bed then. I don't need to take a bath.

Gummy takes a few steps up the hall and confides in me.

> She really does need a bath. She smells.

WE'VE GOT OURSELVES A RUNNER!

Assisted living calls to ask me to call Gummy and tell her that the church meeting she was going on about had been cancelled or changed.

Because she is NOT GOING TO MISS IT dang-nabbit. She's a force to be reckoned with when she decides she's leaving. She packs everything up, and she's good at it. She uses pillowcases and ties her robes and nightgowns into neat little containers that can hold an impressive amount of stuff, especially considering she's a teeny little thing and they aren't very big. Then she straps her purse over her shoulder and marches up the hallway with that expression that struck cold fear into the bowels of each and every one of her boys, and now the assisted living staff.

I call and say that the meeting at the church has been moved to tomorrow. I don't know where in time Gummy is, or if I exist in her life yet, so it is the best I can do.

Please keep in mind there is no church meeting. Her church isn't even in this state.

Then she goes all rational on me, which always catches me off guard.

> Saffi, I only said that because they won't let me out of this
> place. I only wanted to talk to you or my son.

> *Oh.*

> Why won't they let me out of this place?

> *It's ninety degrees outside, Gummy. They probably want
> you in the air-conditioning. Plus it's going to thunder-
> storm. I'm coming over after work and we'll go do some-
> thing fun.*

> Okay.

It does my heart good when she sounds so completely herself for even one more moment.

> But everyone from church is downstairs in the parking lot
> wondering where I am. They're all there. They've been
> waiting for me all day, my dad and Poppy and all of them.

And so we're back to seeing dead people. But we'll have a nice evening. I'll take her out for ice cream and have a nice conversation in which neither of us really knows what we're talking about. Then she'll take a bath with her new bath salts back at assisted living, which will have transformed into some-place else. Probably Burger King again. Last night it was the hospital in her hometown, and she was being held for influenza.

Gummy says she does like it there, but she's not staying. That's the one constant she tells me, at least a couple times a day. One can hardly blame her. She has a life to lead. I'm glad she's not letting dementia stop her from leading it, however Picasso it's gotten. At least there are still moments of sil-ver lining here and there.

WITH GUMMY HERE the shire is starting to feel like home.

This comes as a surprise, although Juan keeps pointing out we've lived here longer than anywhere.

We reminisce about the time Gummy and Poppy watched the kids here while we traveled for business. I remember walking into my bedroom and spotting a huge pile of feathers in a box beside the bed.

> *I don't even want to know what your parents were doing with those.*

My dad was tying flies.

> *Nor do I want to know what that means.*

It's a fishing thing.

> *Whatever. It sounds pretty Fifty Shades to me.*

My kids and the neighbor kids loved when Gummy and Poppy were in charge. They let the kids take turns being boss for the day. That is something parents never want the details of. I do recall the kids' enthusiasm over a huge water fight they'd had.

> *You're kidding me. It's freezing cold outside!*

Don't worry, Mommy. We had it in the house.

chapter twelve

THE EFFING TEACUPS

Assisted living is hosting a huge picnic and most of Gummy's local family is coming. It's a perfect day for it, and it reminds me of all the huge family reunions and church picnics Gummy has been part of during the years. The staff is taking the memory care patients down to the tents together, but Gummy gets to go down early with her family.

She bounds down the steps with enthusiasm. She likes taking the stairs instead of the elevator. In the hallways she passes people in wheelchairs or walkers. They're all people who live in regular assisted living, not memory care. They're senior citizens without memory issues. She's possibly ten years younger than most of them, and she leaves them in her dust.

I go to church with all these people.

You do?

Yeah, don't you recognize them?

They do look familiar.

Today we've planned a big surprise for Gummy. For years she's collected teacups, hundreds and hundreds of them. Juan managed to get a bunch of them brought here to the shire, along with some of her special teacup shelving, and he and the kids are going to hang them up in her room, along with other homey touches from her house.

We're determined to make her comfortable here. It's a nice place. If you have to be in assisted living, it's perfect. Since we first looked at assisted living facilities, I've made it a point to ask people I see in the hallways if they like living in this place. I've yet to have one person say they didn't.

What's not to like? They wait on me hand and foot.

I sure do like it! There's so much to do!

It was boring being at home by myself. This place is a lot of fun.

Have you tried the food? We have a chef!

Outside there's a band playing Woody Guthrie songs. It's Grandparents' Day and they've gone all out. Next to all the tables and tents there are little kids playing soccer. There are mountains of good food, including an ice cream truck. Gummy's smile grows wider and wider as grandkids appear one by one. She points out familiar faces from the memory care unit, both staff and patients, and people she recognizes from day club. She tells us she knows them from her church.

This is her element. Gummy eats corn on the cob, chicken, a hotdog, potato salad, watermelon, ice cream, and peanut butter pie. She washes it all down with soda pop. We're all sufficiently impressed. Throughout the meal she waves at people and makes jokes. She eyes a couple young men carrying in chairs while she takes a sip of her soda.

I could use some hard stuff.

We laugh, not quite certain how far that innuendo goes. She likes it that way. Gummy never drank, and her favorite guy has always been Poppy, but boy does she like to talk smack. For a church lady, she's pretty good at it even now.

Juan and a couple grandkids sneak away to set up Gummy's room.

We go for a walk and watch a soccer game. Gummy makes over every little kid and baby. The conversation becomes circular, full of familiar jokes or a critical remark about a stranger's pants. Real conversation evaporates as the day grows later and conversation skills slip away with the arrival of sundowning. With the help of a granddaughter she finds ancient tricycles in the gazebo beneath her window. They ride them around the courtyard.

How many adults can fit onto a tricycle? Gummy can.

The guys text us a couple hours later and we take her back to her room. She's back at Burger King in her mind until we walk into her room.

Shelves and teacups, knickknacks she painted, and favorite pictures from Gummy's house cover her walls. Even her television, with a remote she understands, is on a stand across from the flowered couch. Gummy stands in the middle of her room and puts her hands on her hips.

> What's this?
>
> We decorated your room! Surprise!
>
> This is my stuff!
>
> Yep.
>
> How'd you get my stuff here?
>
> We brought it to surprise you.
>
> I'm going to have to take this all when I leave.
>
> Don't worry. We'll pack it all up for you when you leave.
>
> Okay. Do you think it's too much? Do you think people are going to say I have too much nice stuff? I don't want them to think I'm showing off.
>
> Oh, I think people are going to like it.
>
> It is nice.

For a few moments she surveys the room and turns to me.

> Do you see all this stuff?

Yes, it's really nice, Gummy.

I brought this all here and hung it up. It was a lot of work.

I can see that it sure was.

It was, but I don't think it's too much.

Neither do I. It's perfect.

The sweating guys are lying on the sofa, laughing.
Life is good. Not easy. But good.

TODAY WHEN I pick up Gummy she says she is *working*. Those delightful aides at assisted living have made her something akin to cruise director. She takes it seriously. She had a great day. Of course half those tea-cups the guys transported across two states safely and hung up? They are down. The woman spends her nights packing.

Despite that it was a good day. She chats the whole time and seems more aware of what is going on than usual. When I take her back to memory care she looks at her tote full of jumbled clothes, teacups and saucers, remotes, and word search puzzles.

When I get mad I do that.

Hallelujah. I doubt anything will come of it, but honesty to oneself must mean something. And I don't blame her for being angry. I do blame her that I have to be the one to put all those flipping teacups back out though. I didn't match them with the right saucer. I only had minutes while she took a bath.

Tonight she can fix them herself. I know her perfectionism won't allow mismatched teacups and saucers.

Tough love.

Teacup version.

I'm hoping she'll be so focused on righting her collection that she doesn't remember to pack to leave.

Hope is the thing with feathers, and mismatched teacups.

NOBODY WOULD ACCUSE me of being an obsessive house-keeper. In fact I'm the opposite. I'd rather write or move than do housework.

However, there are two absolutes. One, the bed must be made.

As soon as I get out I pull the blankets up. That's all it takes because I keep them neat and never mess them up when I sleep. I sleep flat on my back and don't move. Juan is fairly still too, so it works.

Of course he doesn't pull up his side of the bed. It's been a bone of contention. Just do it, I say. And now I add the hundred year argument.

Nothing in marriage is quite as weighty as being able to toss this into the mix.

For one hundred years now, you've said you'll remember tomorrow.

Or.

For one hundred years you haven't pulled up that side of the bed!

I mean it might as well have been one hundred years. Even ten or twenty is a long time. Pull the ding dang blankets up.

But no. Juan doesn't care. Plus, he's powered at least 99% by caffeine and his hearing doesn't work in the morning.

A made bed is highly important. My thinking is spiders don't like to take the time to pull down the blankets and climb in. THAT is why it must be made, and THAT is why no blankets can touch the floor or wall.

I have my reasons.

My second house cleaning thing is my canned food. It must all be stacked neatly in rows, with labels facing forward, like the psycho husband in *Sleeping with the Enemy*. Don't mess it up. No one has to help because only I can achieve canned food perfection. The counters are covered in mail, notepads, keys, books, newspapers, garden tomatoes, purses, pens and pencils et al, but heck yeah, my canned goods cupboard is neat street.

Since Gummy came to the shire, my bed hasn't been made once. All the blankets are twisted chaos. I'm always cold at night now because I've only got a short sheet and one waffle-patterned blanket twisted into a long cold roll. The canned food is a wreck too. I think the symmetry of it stressed Gummy as much as the lack of it stresses me. She will not have it.

She tornadoes through everything.

She doesn't fool with my bed, although despite her being at assisted living I still figure it's only a matter of time before she does. We're visiting or taking her out of there nearly every day, in hopes she'll adjust to that being the home she returns to. But no matter how briefly she's at my house, it's still plenty of time to rearrange the cupboards.

I figure it's good for me. One hundred years is a long time to be a freak about details, although I'm about 99% sure that the spiders of the world have been biding their time waiting for this breakdown in my defenses.

Now that I'm thinking spiders I'll be up until dawn.

FOR THE FIRST time I want to spank her.

I ask the nurse for permission.

Are we allowed to spank them?

She winks.

I could look away for a minute.

I think she feels the same way.

Gummy has taken everything off her walls. I'm talking pictures, sconces, decorations, dozens of teacups AND the big heavy rack screwed into the wall. It took the guys hours to put that stuff up. The aides can't figure out how she reached it.

I know how. She climbed onto the arm of her couch and swung from it like the nimble monkey she is.

Her drawers are a jumble of dirty clothes mixed with clean, notes, cards, newspapers, pencils, books, TEACUPS, fresh flowers, tissues, etc. etc. The place is a wreck.

And she's ranting. Someone's coming in taking her pillows—she counts them—moving her stuff, taking her fifty cent school scissors. I don't humor her. I count the pillows with her and confirm it is the exact number of Target pillows I'd purchased for her. The other stuff? I tell her if she'd stop having tantrums and jamming things into pillowcases and drawers, she'd be able to find it all.

I pick the dirty clothes out, take them to the laundry, and leave everything else as is. Her move.

Misdeeds already forgotten, Gummy is in a good mood, and glad to see me. I brought her a tiny box of chocolates and new slippers. We can't cut the slippers off the little hanger they were attached to, due to lack of scissors. I leave them like that. She likes them enough that maybe she'll hunt for the scissors herself.

We spend a couple hours doing a puzzle in the lounge across from her room. We FaceTime a granddaughter who shows us extended splits and school supplies. Gummy cries a bit because she remembers the girl as much younger, but credits herself for raising such a beautiful young lady.

It turns out to be a nice visit. The people in her memory care unit like her. She's pleasant and animated. She socializes with other patients, and gets them talking, even people who never talk. On the other hand the day club wants to speak with us because there are problems. She doesn't cooperate and mounts coups. I know they went to an apple orchard today to pick apples. I'm not sure what happened. I do know they regularly have to almost drag her back upstairs, because she thinks people are waiting outside to take her home. It's a theme.

By the end of class Gummy has no memory of day club or picking apples. That's the way it rolls. Every day is good, bad, and ugly. It fluctuates from moment to moment.

She's been in this hotel for days doing nothing, she says. It's so boring. She's the only one here. Sunday's picnic is forgotten. Monday dinner at my house has evaporated. The field trip vanished.

But then we walk down the hallway, and Gummy becomes little Miss Hostess.

That's where I go to exercise class at three o'clock. That's where we have church. See that flower garden outside? We walk out there. I like the purple ones. What are they called again? I go to church with that lady.

She waves at a gorgeous woman about her age wearing full makeup and beautiful clothes. I recognize her from day club.

The woman smiles and waves back.

Gummy adds, quite baldly,

She's a bitch.

I'm pretty sure the woman heard. I can only hope she's deaf. If not, she's in memory care too, so I can hope it's not the end of the friendship. Gummy goes on to list all the awful things the woman has done over the years, possibly confusing her with someone real or imaginary. The swearing is completely new. Not to mention malicious gossip. Mostly.

Gummy is no saint, and neither am I, nor the rest of the family. We're regular people trying to make the best of a bad situation. At least the family is. Gummy is trying to get home, where things used to make sense.

AFTER MILLENNIA OF marriage and centuries of children, I thought I understood love. Dementia is teaching me so much more about it. It reminds me of that quote from Alan Bennett in *The Lady in the Van*, "Caring is shit." It's said while he's fussing about the problems with the homeless woman living in a van in his driveway. Low brow as it might sound, I found it rather profound. Shit. You have to put up with a lot of it for love. You give it and you get it. Marketing and movies focus on the pretty parts of love, but there are all sorts of love and a whole lot of it isn't pretty.

Love is hiding in the lounge at assisted living and writing your mother-in-law's name on her underthings so they can be sent to the laundry.

Love is Juan, after weeks of international travel, dragging his jet-lagged bones to assisted living and sorting through the hodgepodge of his mother's clothes, teacups, and papers, and taking down all the wall art he spent hours putting up.

Love is Plan B or C or D or whatever we're on now. It's a Spartan plan. That means no decorations, just a couple boxes of pictures.

Love is realizing that making Gummy's new home like her old one was our ideal. We don't know Gummy's ideal, and she can't remember it.

Love is realizing what used to comfort doesn't anymore. Gummy's been giving her teacups away. She doesn't recognize that they belong to her. She hides them in drawers to keep them safe. Later she panics because they are disappearing.

Love is the nurses and aides who get hit and scratched by patients with dementia, and take it in stride.

Love is adult grandkids who get slapped by a grandmother who's doted on them, and forgive, and comfort their grandmother in her dementia-fueled anger.

Love is people who take time out of their days to spend time with people who suffer from this disease. Especially those who give so much of themselves to Gummy.

I just love her, they say.

Maybe she can't remember their names, but she remembers the love part.

Because people are people and love isn't forgotten, even when particulars are. People suffering dementia still need love. It doesn't look anything like the Hollywood version; it looks like work. Feels like it too.

Real love is messy and hard sometimes, but it's all we've got.

Yes, we love her, and, yes, she's giving us a hell of a lot of shit.

Four hours after I went to bed following a night write, Gummy calls, because she needs a ride home from Burger King.

Argh! Gummy, just go to day club. I'll talk to you later.

I'm not going there. It's boring. My stomach hurts. It's raining and I can't go outside. I'm not going to Sittercise class either. I'm tired of it. I need you to come get me.

I've had almost identical conversations with six-year-olds.

After a couple calls like that, I let them go to voicemail. Dear Hubby and I stop by later. Her favorite aide catches us on the way in.

Hoo boy. She's calling the police today because someone stole all her teacups.

Shit.

chapter thirteen

ORANGE COOKIES

I f someone's legs quit working, and started to shrivel and flop uselessly without any control, would you ever think to say, "Eat better and exercise more. You need to pray more, or better. I've read stories where that works, so I *know* that's how to fix it."

Yes, that's some of the feedback I'm getting.

> My cousin sells vitamins that'll cure Alzheimer's.
>
> Here's a YouTube link about a doctor in New Zealand who can cure dementia *and* Alzheimer's. The AMA is trying to shut him up.
>
> She needs to eat an all vegan diet.
>
> Did you hear about the singer who didn't really have Alzheimer's? It was Lyme disease. I read somewhere that most people really have that. Essential oils can cure it too.

It's borderline cruel, however well intended.

The problem is that the brain is dying. You can't see it like you would legs, but it's dying just the same. Good food, exercise, prayer, and maybe even vitamins might help a person feel better than lack of those important things, but the odds of any of them fixing a dying brain are the same as repairing a couple paralyzed legs.

There are always miraculous stories, and I'm sure some are true—but it does not help to demand a caregiver do things right and produce a miracle. All that does is criticize and come across as sanctimonious. So if that's the goal, by all means, carry on.

AFTER SERIOUS SEARCHING I find Gummy's handwritten orange cookie recipe.

You can tell they taught penmanship when she went to school.

Baking isn't my thing, but Gummy always made these and froze them for visitors.

The search takes me deep into an archaeological dig. My recipe collection is a tactile mess, a trip through history, and cannot be contained.

An entire cabinet in my kitchen is crammed with cookbooks, recipe cards, scraps of papers, and sheets of printer paper filled with random recipes. Whenever we moved I took it all as is and shoved it into the next cabinet, with every intention of going domestic at any moment.

Stand back! It could happen at any time. *insert elevator music here* *or the Jeopardy waiting tune* *forever*

But how cool is it to find recipes from old friends and great-grandparents? In their handwriting too! A hard-drive recipe collection can't compare, plus, I'll never locate those. I have my defunct laptops and hard drives in a similar mishmash pile in my office closet.

Stand back! I'm going to organize all of those! They're full of pictures, all the emails I'm saving, and critically important Pinterest bookmarks.

All the manuscripts I'm writing, have written, or have scrips and scraps of are packed onto USB drives, which I carry with me at all times. You know, in case of computer malfunction, emergency writing sessions while shopping at Target, or an unexpected evacuation of the shire.

I'm ready. Those suckers are locked down and safe.

There might be seventy versions of some novels, but I can sort that out in no time.

Not kidding.

Okay, maybe kidding about sorting them out in no time.

There's something about handwritten notes. They're all unique. I choke up every time I find one of my grandma's recipes with little notes like *Save yourself the time and buy a frozen one*. She was a brilliant woman, far ahead of her time. The Gummy recipe is written on yellow Post-It paper. It goes safely into a plastic baggie and I snap photos of it with my phone, thereby immortalizing it, at least until an x-class solar flare wipes out my electronics.

These are the things you worry about when you carry years' worth of writing on a flash drive in the pocket of your Levi's.

THE ORANGE COOKIES have been baked, frosted, put into freezer bags two by two—so I can take them to Gummy in small batches over time—and photographed, Instagrammed, Tweeted and texted to witnesses who are duly impressed.

Yes. I baked. *cue Hallelujah choir*

They've also been paraded past and taste tested by Juan, who declared them to have too much orange zest. Gummy never made them like that.

It's a wonder I ever make a damn thing for that man or put up with any of his shit.

Remember the comments about *Caring is Shit* in the previous chapter? Isn't it interesting how putting up with someone else's shit is so difficult? As if ours is so much less offensive. It's not like I never give Juan any or—I don't know—write a book about his mom's shit or something.

As I was saying, Gummy likes getting treats. I mean, who doesn't?

I baked! TADA!

What are those?

Your orange cookies!

My orange cookies? I can't bake anymore.

I baked them using the recipe you gave me a long time ago.

What do you want? If you baked for me, you must want something.

It's been helpful throughout this entire ordeal that I know her so well. The problem is that she knows me too. At least she used to, and sometimes still does.

You're so suspicious.

Am I dying?

Only if you criticize them like your son did.

I never said he was very smart.

Right? Well, they're all yours now. He can just starve.

They look good.

I put more orange zest in them than you did. On purpose.

I don't use that. I don't even know what that is.

By the time I got home a swarm of children had already carted off every bag of cookies from the freezer. Miscreants. Juan asked why I told them I baked. He doesn't get the importance of documenting these types of milestones.

EVERY DAY AT 2:05 p.m. my phone rings.

After day club ends, Gummy somehow gets up two flights of stairs and to her room in five minutes.

Sometimes she says she is quitting her job and needs a ride home.

Or she's in the hospital and needs a ride home.

Sometimes she's not sure where she is, but she needs a ride home.

Do you sense the theme?

TODAY IS HARD. The last few days have been great. We had a big family picnic, followed by a family dinner the next day. Don't forget the orange cookies. But these things didn't stay in Gummy's head. She's been in that hospital bored and lonely with nothing to do for days now. Or so goes today's version.

There's no reason she can't go home now, she says. Her car's out of the shop now. So we start our verbal parrying.

> *You need to stay because they're treating your memory problem.*
>
> What are you talking about? I've never seen a doctor.
>
> *Today you're seeing the nurses.*
>
> What nurses?
>
> *The four of them outside your door.*
>
> I didn't see any nurses. Nobody told me about nurses.
>
> *They give you your medicine.*
>
> What medicine?
>
> *The medicine for your memory.*
>
> Nobody gives me medicine.
>
> *In the morning and at night: That tiny white pill. They give it to you in a paper cup, with a little glass of water.*
>
> Is that what that is? It's pretty tiny. I could take that at home.
>
> *But you need somebody with you when you take it. The doctor said.*
>
> What doctor?
>
> *The memory doctor.*

108

I haven't seen any doctor. There's nothing wrong with me,
except my memory. My memory is crap.

Round and round the mulberry bush. The call lasts twenty minutes,
and so does the next one that comes minutes later.

Gummy does have a telephone in her room. It was a choice. Her mind
is a steel trap when it comes to phone numbers. Last week she had someone
in her hometown—who hadn't seen her in ages, or heard what's going on
via the family barking chain—ready to come pick her up at a clinic in a town
near her house. She told them she needed a ride home and they believed
her, until she got to the living at Burger King part.

She can come and go as she pleases in assisted living, but not alone due
to her memory issues. She can call who she likes. I think it's important she
knows she still has freedom. Yesterday we reviewed all her activities for this
week and she lit up.

You mean I'm still going to have a life in this place?

But today she doesn't know what that place is.

TODAY IS ONE of the worst days.

Nothing major happened. Not really.

I get my usual 2:05 p.m. phone call. Remember singing in rounds as
kids? It's like that. Only with Gummy telling me reasons why she has to leave,
and me telling her reasons why she can't. Not yet.

We always say not yet.

I can honestly say to her that when she gets better she can go home.
Her house and car are waiting.

I can honestly hope that is how this will play out.

Hope is the thing with feathers, and no reason, and wishes of chocolate
rabbits and Christmas stockings, and sometimes it works out. We don't look
at it full in the face. We'd go mad. We catch it from the corner of our eyes.

That's why we buy lottery tickets. And start our diet tomorrow. Or give that bad boy we're dating another chance. Hope.

This hope is a cocky bastard. He makes fun of us when we look away, and pulls the dog's tail. But we can't chase him away. He's all we've got.

Still, today is the worst day yet.

In the midst of all the activity I notice.

Maybe I saw clearly at last, sitting in my Jeep on my cell, trying to strike a deal with dementia.

Gummy is insistent. She is going home. She's fine. She's never even seen a doctor here. That hotel she's at doesn't even give her any medicine, ever. Those little white pills they give her? The ones in the paper cups? Oh. Those? She could take those herself. At home.

It's like singing, *Come follow, follow, follow, follow, follow, follow me...* But she can't.

I finally see it.

She can't follow me. She can't go home. She can't drive her car. She can't get better.

Nothing is going to stick.

Nothing is going to matter.

No effort is going to change a thing in the end.

I lose sight of my ugly hope.

Just then Gummy says, okay, she'll give me two weeks and not leave yet. But soon. And a nanosecond later she evaporates again, like that hope. She's leaving. Again. Going home. There was no music therapy today. No, she didn't go to the hair salon. She's sitting in her hotel room all day like always. There are no other people there.

Do you want to sing another round?

Me neither.

But I do.

Because I'd rather smile than cry.

And so would Gummy.

NOT TO BRAG, but there's a good chance I have princess blood.

That's what I thought the first time I saw Juan's family cabin. I mean my hopes were so damn high! There's an A-frame right up the street, and a couple of those cedar sided wonders. But nope. Grandpa built this one, literally, using tar paper and pallets. If you don't know what those are, let me explain. Tar paper looks sort of like asphalt shingles used for roofs, but it comes in large rolls like giant wallpaper. Pallets are flat wooden frames that they put under piles of things in warehouses and shipyards so machinery—I think they're called tow motors—can reach under to lift them up.

The cabin leans to the left. There is an outhouse. Someone nailed antlers to the wall of the front porch. Things went downhill from there. And I'm not a good faker when Juan gestures to each feature like I will someday gesture to my orange cookies. We're in the past here, so I've yet to make any.

Inside the cabin there's a pump. *Inside.* The kind you have to actually pump. The water that comes up is rusty. You have to take an orange bucket to a spring to get good water. The good water comes out of a crack in the hill down the street. I am not entirely comfortable with this idea. There are bats in the walls and chipmunks sneak inside through chinks in the floorboards. The entire place smells like mothballs, which litter the floor. Downstairs is one room, kitchen and living room. As I mentioned, there is no indoor bathroom. Upstairs is also one room, with four beds in it. Apparently that's just ducky when you're there for fishing season, or when you come to sit outside and watch the bears.

According to Juan, feeding the bears is quite a popular activity here (nowadays it's not allowed, but back then anything goes). You can sit outside at night and watch them eat leftovers. I say nothing because my BFF, who married the guy who took her to Mackinac Island for fudge, is at this very moment spending a weekend in Las Vegas. I have no words.

I'm there with my in-laws too. Or at least I will be now, because their car just pulled into the grass beside the "cabin." Parking is on the grass, as there is no driveway. We go out on the porch to greet them. Gummy approaches with a humongous glass jar.

Hi, Gummy. Is that bear food?

No! That's my homemade soup!

That was the best part of that particular weekend. I think there were orange cookies, but I didn't get any. If you call the homemade made-from-scratch soup your new mother-in-law made bear food, you don't get any cookies. Wise up, chica.

It rained the entire week. Nothing much happens at the cabin. It's one of the charms of being there. It's not so charming to have bored family there in bad weather. Gummy and I decided to go out driving for entertainment. That's a thing at the cabin. Going out at twilight to look for animals. Gummy grabbed a bag of Cheetos and off we went. We didn't get very far before I stopped the car and gazed at a field.

What on earth is that?

You're joking right?

Why, what is it? That's the weirdest thing I've ever seen here.

That there's a cow, city girl.

That is not a cow.

Yes it is.

Well, they look different wet.

Won't lie. I'm glad she forgot about that one.

chapter fourteen
500 MILES

This week I am packing my suitcase and following my feet.

That's kind of a bastardized version of a quote from *A Knight's Tale*.

A few weeks after Juan heartlessly tossed me to the Gummy wolves for Singapore, he had to go to Germany. Now I happen to know for a fact that Germany is near Amsterdam and I have *always* wanted to see the Anne Frank house there. I also know for a fact that *someone has piles of airline miles.* As soon as Juan mentions going, I get online to see if I can score Anne Frank House tickets. And. I. Do. I don't know how to get there from Germany, but figure I'll walk the rest of the way if I have to.

So here it is, a month into assisted living, and we ditch Gummy to go on a trip. One thing I've learned after eighty billion years of marriage—when you have an opportunity to do something amazing, you grab it. Carpe diem. Know why? For seventy billion of those years you will pretty much only be doing laundry.

Juan and I leave emergency contact information and Gummy to the capable care of the staff and the rest of the family, and take off to seize some days.

My mind is on the tantalizing fact that I can write while in the hotel in Germany for *three entire days*, and that there is a houseboat in Amsterdam available for an excellent price—and if I can figure out the train schedule I can stay there.

Life has never felt so charmed.

The problem with overnight flights is you arrive at your destination early—their time—and can't check into your hotel, so you sleep in the lobby with an assortment of strangers. And when your room is ready, it is considered the most beautiful room no matter what it looks like.

Just as I fall asleep *finally in my room in Germany*, my phone rings with a call from assisted living. Gummy lost her purse and she's raising the roof. On my last visit before we left, her purse had been sitting in the dining room on a table, Gummy nowhere in sight.

It was stuffed full of notes, pictures in their frames, pens, and a book. It also contained one defunct bank card, her license, and exactly thirteen dollars. Sometimes it gets left behind, and sometimes it is tucked away by its owner, but it is forever going missing. I once found it smashed flat and shoved beneath a stand I'd never imagined it could fit under.

That purse occupies quite a bit of Gummy's time. But if she doesn't have a purse, she will still hunt for it full time in a state of panic. See the dilemma?

The day I found it abandoned on the dining room table in memory care, I led her from her room to the dining room to get it. She tried to formulate reasons the purse was out there. It's a chronic bad scenario. The whole thing is.

In the meantime I'm sleeping in my clothes in front of an open window in Germany. My phone rings. I only half wake to get on the phone with an aide from assisted living. Then one of the hotel staff is at my door. She speaks in vehement German, louder and louder when I don't understand.

Apparently a previous guest left a plastic bag behind. I know this now because someone who speaks English is now calling on the hotel phone while assisted living is on my cell, occupying my other ear. I'm sleepwalking and simultaneously looking for a stranger's bag in my room in addition to Gummy's purse five thousand miles away.

Good morning—or is it night? Not sure because I time traveled. I think I'm ahead of the shire by a good workday. Too bad I can't know where the purse will be found in the past and let them know. Too bad it doesn't work like that.

My kids are keeping Gummy entertained while we're gone. I'm finding it rather entertaining too, because they're texting me long stories.

Let me describe one. Imagine if a couple residents in memory care (also known as Gummy and accomplice) were to see water seeping out from under a door, and burst in as a rescue attempt, only to discover it's bath time.

Our hero rescuers would be mutually horrified and giggling, because, well, naked. Seven, eight, or seventy-eight, this is still cover your mouth and run away laughing worthy.

I appreciate it.

I am the most thrilled by the news that Gummy has a partner in crime, however briefly. She's found someone else in memory care to hang out with, someone to help her keep order and go on rescue missions when necessary. It's nice to think life goes on, and however hobbled it may be, it still counts.

The dark trench coat and black boots might have been an excellent investment because people have been addressing me in German all day. Yes, this is a good thing. I don't know how, but locals seem to always spot an American right off. You walk toward them and suddenly they're speaking in English.

I make an effort to go incognito. No sneakers. No fanny pack (yes, the American said fanny pack). No purse, just mystery money that appears magically in my hand if I decide to buy something.

If only I spoke German this could work.

Gummy hasn't called me yet. Someone else does, because she called *them* and said she was in jail for stealing *candy*.

She asked him to come bail her out.

This disease is an evil bastard. For such a clever woman to ever utter that nonsense, and straight up believe it, is full-on bullshit.

Still, I do see the humor in it. Gummy would too if she was herself. We'd roll around cracking up like we did that time we cleaned out her in-laws' house after they died. Her mother-in-law had an impressive collection of antique sanitary pads. By our estimates they were approaching sixty years old. Cash had been tucked into the weirdest places, like inside those old-fashioned roller blinds. We'd roll down a blind and a few twenties would flit out.

We both pointed out that this would not be a thing for us, as we both intended to spend all available cash before our demise.

I meant it, because here I am in Germany on a random September day, buying fresh blackberries, wiener dog keychains with silver feet, and some sort of pastry made of almond paste and God's blessings. I'm recharging quickly. It's amazing what a few thousand miles between you and your problems will do.

Today I'm perfectly content with having left the business world to write. I mean, right now I'm playing and not writing, but poor Juan is stuck in back-to-back meetings. When we had our own little engineering company, I had to work during these business trips too, and couldn't go incognito in foreign countries. The concept of going incognito reminds me of Gummy. The only place she goes is wherever her brain slams her at any given moment, and her true identity is concealed by traitorous proteins in her brain. This is who we are now. Incognito. However lucky, unlucky, half-assed or unfair it is.

P.S. Gummy claims she is innocent of all candy stealing charges.

IT'S MIDNIGHT IN Germany and my favorite Gummy just called—because her phone skills are excellent, and believe you me she remembers my number—to tell me she got the paperwork ready for the kids, and what should she do with it?

What paperwork? What kids?

The phone is going on mute for the night. Although my favorite Gummy could math you up one side and down the other, she can't fathom I'm somewhere in another time zone. Well, actually she can, but only long enough for this exchange:

> You're where?
>
> *Germany, Gummy. Juan's here on a business trip.*
>
> Nobody told me!

And reset.

It's 1:30 a.m. in Germany, and my not-so-favorite Gummy just called again—and mute doesn't mean crap with these phones because it vibrates quite loudly against the bedside table. Yes, boys and girls, it's sundowning time in the shire time zone, but that doesn't interfere with her phone skills, not one little bit.

> Saffi, it's Gummy. I need a favor.
>
> *What's going on?*
>
> Well, I'm stuck at Burger King without a car and I need a ride home.
>
> *Gummy, I'm in Germany.*
>
> It won't take very long.
>
> *It will because I'm in GERMANY, the country. In Europe.*
>
> What? Nobody told me!

I put the phone on the floor and put my backpack over it.

It's 2:00 a.m. in Germany and my backpack is buzzing. I unbury it and hit the ignore button. After it goes to voicemail I call assisted living and talk to the switchboard operator. All calls have to go through the switchboard. They understand time differences. Gummy's calls to me are now on lockdown.

Is that the Alamo?

No, Poppy.

It looks like the Alamo.

I thought you'd never been there. How do you know what it looks like?

I saw the movie. Is that one over there the Alamo then?

Gummy pipes up from the backseat, interrupting him.

Knock it off, Poppy. You're not funny.

We've been driving for hours! How long does it take to get there?

Forever.

Of course I don't say that out loud. Due to some horrific thing I did in a former life, I'm driving across Texas with my in-laws in the back seat so they can see the flipping Alamo. I lost my will to live somewhere around Austin. Only a few million more light years to go. This is purgatory. This is my atonement for all the things. I have to pee but refuse to stop this car for any reason that will involve adding even a nanosecond to this trip.

Is that the Alamo?

Sitting in the passenger seat, Juan serenely looks out the window. When we were first married and he'd zone out like this, I used to wonder and worry where his mind was. Now I'm one hundred percent certain it's some sort of survival white noise trance that men are gifted with.

More than I wish I could stand and pee, I wish I had been gifted with that white noise trance that protects me from that which I do not want to deal with.

Sure Juan managed to take time off work to spend with his parents, but with the itinerary of a college football game, the effing Alamo *if* I don't implode first, and then a Near Year's Day bowl game in Houston. Yes, I am driving all over the great state of Texas *with the in-laws.*

They're mad I brought a book to read at the games.

Apparently this is fun. I always thought fun would be more fun than this.

IN ADDITION TO visiting us no matter where we moved, Gummy sometimes sent plane tickets to the kids and me to come and visit. They always went all out, taking the kids to picnics or amusement parks. It blew my mind that they'd ride the coasters with them. I stood at the exit to the ride holding soft drinks, hats, and glasses. When they exited, windblown and with nothing nice to say about the latest advances in upside-down roller coaster technology, they'd still get right back in line if the kids wanted to go again.

They took pictures and bought tickets, inviting extended family and friends, including mine. If I wanted to go to a high school reunion or hang out with my girlfriends, they were more than willing to babysit. When the kids wanted special Halloween costumes, Gummy sewed and arranged a special place for Beauty and the Beast in the local Halloween parade.

When I fussed to friends about another impending in-law visit, they both sympathized and envied. It didn't take me long to notice Gummy and Poppy were the *best* grandparents.

FOR THE FIRST time in our bazillion year marriage we had extra money at Christmas. We decide to spend it on Gummy and Poppy. The next summer we take them with us on our annual portage deep into the Canadian bush, where they can all ride around in boats and *fish*, while the kids zip around the little sandbar island, and beneath mosquito netting I write to the hum of a generator *as much as I want because meals are served in the lodge! Kids are with grandparents! No cooking! No cleaning!*

Nature.

Quiet.

Writing.

My life is charmed. And did I mention Gummy and Poppy are in the cabin *next* to ours, which really isn't that close. Once or twice during the week I sacrifice some time and go out in the boat with them—and take a book.

When Gummy heads out in the boat, at least one of the kids stays behind to booby trap her cabin. They've been short-sheeting her bed all week and she's never said a word about it. After an evening spent brainstorming, the kids are planning to step it up a notch. I'm pretty sure this will involve crackers in my in-law's pillow cases.

It's our last vacation together, but we don't know it at the time. We don't think much when Gummy has a late night attack of confusion that Poppy calls the *hee-hee gee-bees*. We don't ask questions even when he says that there's something really wrong with Gummy. Only in retrospect after he's gone will we even remember it.

They head back home a few days before we do, and we stand at the dock and wave goodbye. It went well, but we're just as happy to have time to ourselves. We're really glad we did this, but the real vacation starts now.

Meanwhile in the here and now in Germany, I sleep soundly and slip into another real vacation.

chapter fifteen

THAT'S NOT VERY LADYLIKE

The worst part about holidays, weekends, and vacation is always the same thing: when the bill comes due. It's always way more than you expect. I get to Amsterdam at long last, stay in a houseboat with portholes and swans peeking through them, and tour the Anne Frank house. We manage the entire thing on a reasonable budget too. But when I get back to the shire, the real cost becomes due.

The first day back Gummy has an eye doctor appointment. This is what I've been waiting for. Remember she saw dead people at the cemetery? I hope it is because of her glasses. It isn't, but I don't know that yet and cling to my false hope.

My other false hope is the excitement and anxiety of seeing her again. After settling her into assisted living for a short month, we'd taken off. I am desperate to see her again and hopeful that this will be a sign we've done the *right thing*.

When I buzz myself into the memory care unit, a few more people than Gummy are waiting for me.

The first person I see is Gummy, because she's always standing by the door clutching her purse filled with whatever treasures she's planning to use in her new hobo life after escape.

Two RNs wait with paperwork and issues to discuss.

One caseworker needs to talk about Gummy's exit-seeking and violent behavior.

One psychiatrist waits to be introduced, as he is their suggested fix for helping Gummy with her behavior.

Two of the aides on duty that she's assaulted today want to explain what happened.

One of the off-duty aides who loves her is also waiting, having stayed to champion her. She believes although Gummy *can* attack like a wyvern launching from the top branches of a tree doesn't make her a bad person.

There are also two other memory care patients waiting. They've chosen to become Gummy's minions and help her storm the castle whenever it is needed.

Those in charge want to impress upon me that Gummy's medication needs to be increased so she stops opening up cans of whoop-arse on staff. They've been calling the doctor's office for two days. *If* Gummy doesn't stop launching herself at nurses like that alien thing with the tentacles that attach to your face, she could be out. Expelled.

If she knew that, she'd be all over them tonight, until the place looked like the ending of a Quentin Tarantino movie. Her only goal in life is to go home and return to her normal life. She can't remember that if she gets tossed out of the memory care unit of assisted living, she'll be on lockdown in a nursing home.

Out of the frying pan and into the fire.

As much as I'd like the personal satisfaction of sitting her down and lecturing her about consequences until her ears bled, there's no point. It'd be like demanding a newborn stop filling diapers. Gummy isn't a newborn. She's a clever adult with the life experience of over seven decades. The only problem with her is ZERO RECALL.

She'd swear on a Bible and her life that she never hit anyone, and think I'm whacked for saying it, and that the entire cast and crew of assisted living are evil assassins plotting her demise, which would only increase her panic to get out of there.

The worst part of not being able to remember is when you can't remember that you can't remember. That's when you've entered the Twilight Zone. It's a whole new ballgame at that point.

And how much did Gummy miss me?

Where have you been?

Juan and I were in Amsterdam.

You should have told me you were going to be late. I've been waiting for you since last night.

The very aides she's assaulted today help search her room for her glasses, digging through drawers and pillow cases crammed with all the bits and pieces that she's squirreled away for nuclear winter. The glasses are nowhere to be found.

One aide freezes mid-search. "WAIT!" She ducks down, looks under the bed and pulls Gummy's glasses out. "That's where they'd be if it was one of my kids," she says.

In the two hours that follow at the eye doctor, I'm not sure anyone noticed Gummy had a memory problem. She's an excellent faker. She follows an impeccably dressed well-heeled woman down the hallway, imitating her wiggly walk with impressive precision. It would have made a middle-schooler proud. I force myself to choke down a laugh so as not to encourage her. Suddenly I feel more like the parent than ever before.

Gummy blazes through her eye exam and gets to choose new glasses. She has her eye on a bejeweled pair of Prada glasses for a whopping $585, before lenses. I nix that like I'm the mom again, whispering to the woman helping us that they'll be lost or crushed within two months, if not sooner.

For the first time Gummy recognizes assisted living when we return. She does *not* want to return, but we walk through the flower gardens and past the gazebo and discuss the fact that it is dinner time and the food at this place is pretty darn good.

She asks if she can't go live with one of her sons in her hometown. I say the problem with that is they're never home.

That's good! I don't want to have to see them all the time.

But the problem is you can't be alone.

Why not?

You have a memory problem.

I know I have a memory problem, Saffi. But I can sit in my own house and I'll be fine. I want to go back there.

The doctors don't want you to go back there.

Throwing the doctors under the bus comes even before Juan now.

I don't care what the doctors say.

Legally I don't think we can let you go back home alone.

I'm not sure if that's accurate, but I'm positive it'd be morally wrong.

Then I'll go live with my dad.

I think he passed away fifty years ago. In the end Gummy becomes bored with my lame responses and joins her minions for dinner so they can plot and plan whatever will have the staff calling me later tonight.

AFTER WE FIRST moved to the shire, Gummy and Poppy came for most holidays and special occasions. Like the first day of fishing season. Or if the kids were doing anything that could be deemed *cute* by grandparents. One day that stands out in my memory, I had two little girls in my living room. One mine. She was lying upside down on the couch with her legs in the air, attempting to do some type of aerial split. "That's not very ladylike!" her friend shouted, before plopping herself on the couch with her little behind sticking up. My daughter bellowed, *"That's* not very ladylike!"

I stayed in the kitchen digging through the trash. Gummy kindly peeled ten pounds of potatoes for dinner and I suspected she had accidentally thrown the utensils away with the peelings. It didn't seem portentous or out of the norm at the time. Don't we all do that stuff? The girls ran into the kitchen. My daughter grabbed two of Gummy's orange cookies and rammed them both into her mouth at once, and proceeded to chew, mouth open, as bits dropped out. Her friend watched intently, announcing, *"That's* not very ladylike!"

The other girl proceeded to suck down a soft drink so fast it sounded like a drain. She stopped drinking and opened her mouth for an impressive burp. My daughter danced in place with giggling enthusiasm.

That's not very ladylike!

Girls! What the heck are you doing?

We're playing the Gummy game!

What are you talking about?

Instead of answering, my daughter jammed a finger up her nose. Gummy walked into the kitchen.

Get your finger out of your nose! That's not very ladylike.

The girls cracked up laughing and zipped out of the kitchen, and I started laughing too. Before then I'd never really thought about the fact that Gummy said those words all the time. Years later, when my daughter's friend has long since moved away, my daughter texts her a picture of Gummy purposely sitting spread eagle or *like a slob,* as Gummy often says. *That's not very ladylike,* the caption reads. Gummy finds it hysterical.

Well, it's not very ladylike!

Dear Doctor,

Gummy is in assisted living now. She's having a lot of trouble knowing where she is and what's going on most of the day, and she's taken to assaulting staff.

I did speak with her about attacking people, but she has no recollection within seconds of doing it. I think she goes after those who tell her things she doesn't want to hear or can't handle. She has a tendency toward playful threats and swats, but it can now turn rather abruptly.

She's also tearing things off the walls and still packing to leave. They consider her a flight risk.

Help.
Saffi

They double her medications.

Prescription drugs are my nemesis but I'm fully behind this plan.

They always ask first.

I'm more than a little terrified that assisted living will kick her out. As fit and trim and active as she is, I can't bear the idea that she'd go into a nursing home at such a young and healthy age.

VHS VIDEOTAPES WERE once a new thing. During one such visit, Gummy cracked up because she asked one of the kids—not much more than toddlers at the time—to bring her tape. He brought her a videotape. She wanted Scotch tape.

Once the kids go down for a nap, Gummy and I sprawl out in my Texas-sized living room and prepare to do an exercise tape together. We kick our shoes into a corner.

Are these your shoes or Juan's?

Thanks, Gummy. They're mine.

They're huge! What size shoe do you wear?

Tens now. I grew a size with each kid.

If you have any more kids, you're going to have to wear the boxes.

Probably.

When I was young, ladies wore size five or six.

Well, I think prenatal vitamins work well on feet.

You couldn't be big back then. Not if you wanted to get married.

The tape is starting. You have to get on your hands and knees and lift your leg up like this.

That's not very ladylike.

Give me a break. You played football when you were a kid.

With the neighbor kids!

Were you very ladylike at it?

No. But my mother yelled at me for that.

WE MAKE IT back to the eye doctor to pick up Gummy's new glasses. I take a picture of her in them and show it to her.

Can you get me a copy of that? It makes my boobs look bigger.

One thing dementia has taught me is that we don't outgrow insecurities. I guess we bury them.

When we walk into the memory care unit, an aide notices her glasses right off.

Look at you, Gummy. Nice glasses!

You like those? I look sexy, don't I?

She laughs and rolls with it.

You always look good!

Are you hitting on me? Because I'm a married woman.

Gummy flounces down the hall, wiggling her hips a bit and chuckling.

When Gummy first went into the memory care unit of assisted living, I thought that the monthly rent was defense budget insane.

A bit more than a month later, I'm thinking it's not so bad.

The staff in memory care are Juan's new idea of superheroes.

Imagine trying to corral four Gummy's!

And there are about ten Gummy's in each unit.

There's a message on the answering machine from Gummy by the time I get home from assisted living. I call her back.

Hey, Gummy-Gummy, what's up?

Oh, I'm so glad you called. I need to go home.

I don't think anyone can come get you right now.

Why not? I just got off of work.

I think everyone else is still at work right now.

Nobody told me. I guess I can walk, but it's raining right now.

Don't walk. It's going to thunderstorm.

You don't sound very good.

I'm coming down with a cough.

You should go to the doctor.

Maybe I will.

You don't have to call me all the time, you know.

Okay, Gummy. I won't.

THERE IS A new patient on the floor who is keeping the caseworker and staff quite occupied, so Gummy looks tame by comparison.

Now that's scary.

What they need at assisted living is the holodeck from Star Trek. That's the only solution I can come up with.

Passes that brilliance on to the engineers in the crowd.

That way each person could live in whatever reality keeps them calm at the moment. Trying to drag them into our reality isn't working. They end up dragging us into theirs.

Too much of my day is spent trying to worm Gummy out of her delusion and garner her cooperation.

I'm quitting this place and going home.

Okay.

Will you drive me?

You can't go home until the doctors say you can.

I don't care what the doctors say. Why can't I?

You have to be with someone because of your memory.

Then I'll just go live with my dad. Is he still in that house?

I'm not sure where your dad's house is.

It's never a matter of telling Gummy the bald truth anymore. It won't fit. It's more a matter of easing her closer and closer to reality, in microscopic increments that won't wreck her. I can feel her anxiety. I can sense that any answers to her questions will upset her. My modus operandi is distraction.

We can have real moments without the pain of too much information. Think about trying to feed a baby a vegetable they don't like. You try distraction. *Look at the airplane!* You try stealth, a bit of green mush on the spoon of applesauce. You try bald-faced lying. *Yum! Yum! Mommy loves liquefied green beans!*

It's pretty much the same thing. I'm lying to someone I love because I want to keep her safe. I want her to thrive. I want her to be happy.

> *You can't walk home tonight. It's raining and cold.*
>
> *No, I haven't seen Poppy tonight, but it's hunting season.*
>
> *Even if you can't go home right now, we could go to the park! Do you want to go to the park?*
>
> *Let's just get out of here for a while. We can go for a drive, roll the windows down, and turn the radio on full blast.*

There's still plenty of room for joy. It's a matter of figuring out how to get it in there.

Since I have a wicked cold and fever and never got out of my pajamas today, I decide not to visit Gummy. She calls and tells me to get her out of the hospital and take her home right now.

> *I can't right now, Gummy.*

Thanks for nothing.

She hangs up on me.

I slip into that *mom-oh-no-you-did-not* mode and call her right back. Since they changed her medication, she has become a real firecracker.

> *Gummy? What are you doing?*

Oh, I'm giving them hell.

> *Why?*

Because I'm not staying in this hospital. Why can't I go home?

We do the verbal dance, always circular with only a few variations. She's never seen a doctor once since she got there! She doesn't know what I'm talking about!

This time I'm tired. I can't breathe. My throat is sore, and my patience is too. I break the rule of dementia. I say *remember*.

> *Except the day before yesterday. Remember? We sat on the couch together at the doctor's office. The nurse had dimples and pretty hair. Remember how pretty she was? And the doctor wore a blue flowered dress. She rubbed your neck.*

That's right, she was nice.

Either Gummy does remember, or she is rolling with my story. Who can tell? Anyway, she calms down, and it becomes today's little miracle. After twenty more minutes of circular debate, she agrees to put up with this crap for me until I feel better.

I tell her to go get her hair done because she looks like a hobo. She has been refusing to go to her appointments, hell bent on escaping. She never thinks to ask how I know what she looks like over the phone, and agrees to go now.

God bless vanity. At least she still has that.

I don't know if she will go or not.

Maybe she'll forget as soon as we hang up. I try calling back later, but she left the phone off the hook. She's been doing that for a couple years. She misses the cradle.

Once, years ago, when her mother-in-law went into a nursing home, Gummy asked me to promise that when her time came I'd keep her presentable, and pluck her chin hairs if necessary. I promised. She has no chin hairs. I really wish it could be that simple.

chapter sixteen

TOO SEXY

Gummy crawls into my Jeep a bit slower than usual. For a moment I worry she'll fall back out, and I put my hands on her rear to steady her.

You like that, don't you!

I bought a Jeep just so I could do this.

I'm pretending to have dementia just so you can too.

I almost fall down laughing. Somehow I manage to get her backend into the seat. Every now and then she makes a memory joke. They always catch me off guard. I shut her door and hop into the driver's seat, still chuckling, but her mind has moved to the seatbelt. She's having trouble clicking it. I want to help but hesitate. Reaching over and buckling her seatbelt might upset her. It might be too much. It hasn't been that long since she was buckling seatbelts for grandkids.

Do you need a hand, Gummy? That belt is tricky.

After all these years you'd think I'd know where the hole is.

Er…

Sometimes Poppy had trouble with it.

132

We're sitting in my Jeep right by the front door of assisted living and I'm crying with laughter.

Gummy remembers where the hole is, and off we go.

Where are we going?

To the doctor.

What doctor?

Your memory doctor.

Nobody told me! I look like a hobo!

You look fine, Gummy.

I hope I don't have to take my clothes off. I didn't shave my legs.

It's the doctor, Gummy. Not a date.

What am I going to the doctor for?

Your memory.

My memory is crap. There's nothing they can do though.

They have medicine for it.

Does it work?

It's worth a try, isn't it?

At least I'll finally get to meet this memory doctor.

There's no point in telling her she's met this doctor. Many times.

Are you hungry?

I'm starved.

The aides had informed me Gummy had gotten tossed out of adult day club today, and missed lunch because she had a revolution to plan. So I give her the emergency little bag of Doritos and a Pepsi I keep on hand for her at all times. It's Gummy Nip.

Gummy has gained ten pounds since we got her. She gapes at the number on the scale.

Fick it. I'll fick it.

The nurse looks at me.

That's how one of the grandkids used to say fix.

Gummy laughs.

He ficked everything with a hammer too. Remember that part?

The doctor decides to stop one medicine because it could be contributing to the outbursts of violent behavior. We're not counting the hammer on the scale comment as violence. I think that feeling is normal.

The doctor also agrees to run a Lyme disease test. Among all those random private messages from people I don't know on social media, one was about how dementia is really Lyme disease. Of Gummy's siblings still living, several of them have memory problems. I realize that mathematically the odds of them *all* having Lyme are unlikely. But what if? I know it's unscientific and a long shot and likely should get tossed into the same bin with people who send me links for essential oils that'll cure Alzheimer's. But I'm leaving no stone unturned here.

I call the pharmacy to see if Gummy's new prescriptions will be ready tonight, and they say no and that they are closing. Then the pharmacist pauses and asks if we need it tonight. I explain the situation, and the pharmacist offers to fill it and take it to assisted living on her way home.

The shire is a great place to live.

You think you don't want to live in a small town in the middle of nowhere, but there are benefits to it. Plus there are roads in and out, and normally they're unguarded, so you can leave if it gets on your nerves.

Gummy doesn't know the shire is a great place to live, because she can't keep track of where she is anymore. By the time we're back at my house for dinner, she's back to never having met the memory doctor again.

I like your Jeep, but I don't know how to get in or out of it.

I'm helping her out, and she's moving much slower than usual.

Are you dizzy, Gummy?

No. I'm tired. My legs are weak.

We should have told the doctor!

What doctor?

The memory doctor. We were just at the doctor's.

What are you talking about?

I change the subject.

I'm talking about the fact that I made you dinner and put it in the crockpot today. Are you hungry?

No. I ate something earlier.

You might think that's the fault of the Gummy nip, except she ate half of one Dorito and had two sips of soda, and that took her the entire drive to the doctor to accomplish.

You know I don't make sauerkraut for anyone but you.

I'm stuffed full.

But I actually cooked! For you!

Sorry. Nobody told me.

Where did you eat a big lunch?

My sisters and I went somewhere. I forget. I had a fish sandwich and French fries.

Despite Gummy's imagined lunch with her sisters, when she sits down for dinner, she eats. Afterwards she spends time with grandkids and scours the house for good stuff. Of course she finds the freak-fracking-mofo-plucking ding-dang teacups we had taken down a while back. She tosses them into totes and tries to take them with her.

She's never boring. And now I hope for good results with the new pills, and maybe a miracle cure with the test.

I'm a fiction writer. If I was writing this reality, it could happen.

TONIGHT IS THE first time I've been over to see Gummy in a few days. I've been completely preoccupied producing mucus. When I walk in she is waiting right by the door. Like a raptor looking for holes in the electric fence, she's always testing her latest escape strategy.

Here's MY RIDE!

Here's your FAVORITE daughter-in-law.

You're not Samantha.

Funny monkey.

The staff loves her, even the ones she's gone after and scratched up during escape attempts. She's sassy. Two of them follow me out tonight to tell me Gummy had instigated a late night conversation yesterday. She had the women all huddled together laughing, discussing the night they'd lost their virginity.

Imagine that conversation in the memory care unit. I'd have paid to be there for that.

I've brought Gummy her hometown newspaper, cards from friends, a piece of pumpkin roll—which is her favorite thing on earth, thank you, Wegmans—and two jackets sent from Gummy's house. We settle down and work on a puzzle we started a couple days ago. We'd left it finished, but she tore it apart and packed it up in one of her tirades. She doesn't remember we've done it before, and you'd think I'd be faster at it because I do, but no. Puzzles aren't my thing. But I'm sure if they were my thing, I could do them faster than every single person in the memory care unit. Or at least *one* of them.

Gummy quizzes the residents here, certain she knows them from her hometown. A woman today held firmly to the fact that she was from *here*. It's interesting to listen to them speak. Their personalities seem very much intact, but whatever part of our brains keeps us aware of our surroundings is muddled. Neither Gummy nor her fellow memory care mate are quite sure where they are now or why. The other woman is far more accepting of this fact. Gummy is not accepting. She doesn't really care where she is, because she's leaving anyway. Before I leave I run her a bath, put her pajamas in the bathroom, and try to point her in that direction.

You're not coming in there with me are you?

No, Gummy.

Good, because I don't like anybody checking out my body unless they're going to appreciate it.

I appreciate your body, Gummy. You take the stairs faster than I do.

Even as I say it, it hits me that it isn't true anymore. She's getting slower, both with eating and moving.

I don't swing that way, you know, and I'm married.

Okay, Gummy, but get in there while the water's still hot.

Gummy sashays into the bathroom singing.

Hot. Hot. Hot. I'm bi-texy for my shirt, bi-texy for my shirt, bi-texy!

Gummy is one of those grandparents who picked up every funny mispronunciation her grandchildren ever made and incorporated it into her vocabulary. I might be slightly guilty of doing this with my kids when they were little too. It's also possible that this is a thing Gummy and I did together at certain points in time.

MY TODDLERS IN the backseat are vying for Gummy's attention.

Gummy, there's no flag boats on the motion today.

As we drive past the water, she looks from her grandkids to me for parental interpretation.

Sailboats on the ocean.

You're right, sweetie, there aren't any flag boats on the motion. I think it's going to thunderstorm so the flag boats probably got off the motion.

It's gonna wain, Gummy. We need a humbrella.

I brought a humbrella, so let it wain!

It does rain. We're driving home from the petting zoo, crossing a long bridge when the heavens open up. This is Texas, and the rain comes down like a waterfall. Thunder vibrates through the van and lightning zigzags across the sky sideways. Gummy crawls into the backseat to sit between two car seats, and sings. The kids adore Gummy's singing. She sings the best songs, and the same lyrics they do.

The wheels on the bus go wound and wound, wound and wound, wound and wound...

It's tornado weather. I slow the van, but don't stop on the bridge. This is the last place you want to get stuck if the weather turns dangerous. I hate this bridge. Now and then people go off it into the water. It's a mother's nightmare. The wind buffets the van as we cross in near zero visibility. Fortunately, the road is straight and I could probably drive it with my eyes closed. It kind of feels like I am.

The dwiver on the bus goes moob on back, moob on
back, moob on back...

Maybe we shouldn't have gone out today, but it's Gummy's last day
here, and the kids love the petting zoo. Oh, who are we kidding? I do too.
Gummy had a blast also. Today she protected the kids from angry geese, sat
in a tractor with them, and patted a baby pig while talking about the pet one
she had as a little girl.

The peoples on the bus go wup and drown, wup and
drown, wup and drown.

Last week a funnel cloud went right over our house as we got ready for
pee-wee soccer. Juan watched it while I hauled the kids back inside to hud-
dle in an interior room, despite the oldest one's protests not to forget I was
snack mom. Oddly enough I reassured myself with math. Texas is a big state.
Odds are in my favor. But that F5 one that hit makes me antsy...I don't know
it at the time, but it always will.

The horn on the bus goes bee—MOM! DO IT!

This is the driver participation part of the song. Moving at a crawl we
drive through town and I beep the horn in all the right spots. With the Arma-
geddon storm going on outside I could hardly hear it. When we finally got
home and pull into the garage, it took me a moment to peel my hands off the
steering wheel. The kids protested.

That was fun, Mommy! Let's go get fri-fries!

Gummy sided with them.

Yeah, Mommy! Let's go get fri-fries!

Mommy is not going back out in that storm for French fries!

Gummy leaned forward from the back seat.

It's just a wittle wain, Mommy! We have a humbrella!

EVERY NOW AND then Gummy will tell me a far-fetched tale that turns out to be completely true. It pleases her so much when I tell her later how she was right about who is dating whom, or some wild news tidbit.

> *When you told me that I thought NO WAY, but once again you were right!*

I are smart.

She loves to joke, but worries about being considered stupid. It's a crushing blow to someone as clever and social as she's always been.

> *Of course you're smart.*

Right.

> *I'm serious, Gummy. You have a memory problem. That doesn't make you stupid.*

I can't remember crap.

> *You have bad times and good times, but you're still smarter than the average bear.*

Of all the things I tell her, I swear it's when I tell her that she was right that she remembers best. Perhaps we all remember those times we were right. Or maybe it's because it's juicy gossip, or because the more she hears the same information repeated in slightly different ways, the better chance it will penetrate.

Gummy is not all the way gone. We never know what's going to get stuck in her sails at any given time though. It's like her brain is sailing over everything that's ever happened to her—all clouded by her perspective and crippled ability to recall. We all do that anyway, right? We only have our own minds to count on. Therefore *all* memory is fallible.

I'm driving and Gummy calls in tears. She tells me all the awful things someone said to her over the phone, and I sit in the parking lot of the super-market and have her repeat it again and again. Together we pick apart each insult, looking for the sense in it.

> *Now you know how much she loves you. Why would she say that?*
>
> I don't know. She was so mean.
>
> *What did she say exactly?*
>
> That I'm lazy and just have to lie around all day now.

What started as a terrifying betrayal slowly shrinks to misunderstanding and perspective where it belongs. Gummy tries to go back to the original version and I reassure her again.

> *Now you know how much she loves you. Why would she say that?*
>
> I don't know. She was so mean.
>
> *What did she say exactly?*
>
> That I'm lazy and just have to lie around all day now.

Maybe it didn't really penetrate. Maybe she just got bored with our con-versation. Maybe the entire thing never happened at all. Maybe she dreamed it. It doesn't matter much when it's real to her. But eventually she stops being afraid, and decides she wants to watch a hurricane on the news, and she will talk to me later.

I call that a win.

Those wins are hard won.

Some days I'm the Gummy Whisperer.

Mostly I'm desperate.

THE DOCTOR DID get back to me to let me know Gummy doesn't have Lyme. Just plain old incurable dementia.

They told me that was good. I'm trying to believe them.

When I arrive at assisted living today, Gummy is in the lounge with all the other residents watching Cocoon.

Doesn't that sound stereotypical?

I don't immediately recognize the back of her head against so many other white ones, because she had her hair done today. It's obvious they all use the same stylist.

I take her back to my house for soup—her old vegetable soup recipe. The one I once thought was bear food. I'm glad she's forgotten about that.

At least I think she has.

Probably not. I'm sure it's floating around in there somewhere.

During soup and pie, Gummy is chatty and happy, but has to get back early because tonight is bonfire night and they are having a sing-along *and* s'mores.

By the time we head back everything has evaporated and she is sundowning. She has no idea there is a bonfire, or sing-along, or s'mores.

It's impossible to completely describe sundowning, probably because it's different for everyone. I can see it in Gummy's eyes. It's like looking at someone who's had too much to drink or is on drugs. It's not a wide pupil thing. It's a vacancy thing. Sometimes she's in there floating around, and sometimes she's near impossible to reach.

Even when she's *with it*, she might think she's at work or living in a mall, or both. In the evenings she seems more like a sleepwalker, or caught in a dream. She goes through motions and responds, but she's always somewhere else.

The shire is stunning right now with the leaves changing. On our way back we crest the top of a hill. Thousands of Starlings are doing their murmuration against the sunset. Black birds against yellow sky. They swoop and move as one, like a dark dancing cloud they weave into patterns and shapes, twisting and turning against the sunset. We stop and she watches, transfixed.

It is so beautiful here I might want to live here with you.

I could live with that, Gummy.

I think tonight's sundowning was a good dream for both of us.

chapter seventeen

NEVER ENDING STORY

The day started off bad.

When I arrive at assisted living, Gummy's door is shut and she is lying on her bed crying.

I'd rather have to pull her off a nurse.

I try to comfort and reassure her, and as she explains her tears, she seems all there. Missing grandchildren. Her life. Her mind. All justifiable reasons to lie down and cry.

As fate would have it, the caseworker calls. He has the psychiatrist with him, and I am invited to stay for the evaluation.

Why is it that a deep philosophical discussion with a psychiatrist is such a cathartic experience for me? There are tears and laughter for all three of us, and I have a strangely good time. So does Gummy.

I'm not even sure what all we talk about. He tells us about himself, and we tell him about us. I tell him how we dragged Gummy away from her perfectly good life to live here in the shire so we can try to help her with her memory problems. It is news to Gummy, but she adds plenty. She wants to go home. The last few years have been rough, because she's been forgetting things and gets lost, but she thinks she does okay—or would, if we'd just leave her in her own house.

He asks if I work. People assume I don't when I'm hanging around assisted living at two o'clock in the afternoon. When I say I write novels, he asks Gummy if I should write one about her.

> I don't know about that. You never know what she'll say.
>
> What if she gives you all the money?
>
> In that case she can write whatever she wants to.

When he leaves Gummy walks him to the door.

> He's a nice guy. He's from my church. He comes by here
> to visit and we just talk and laugh the whole time.
> *I liked him.*
>
> Me too, but Poppy goes and sits on the back porch when
> he comes and won't come inside until he leaves.

That visual made me laugh and wonder if something like that had happened. I can picture it. I'm pretty sure my Spock-ish engineer husband wouldn't consider time spent with a psychiatrist evaluating his mother a good time either. Oh, well. Gummy and I liked it.

USEFUL LIFE TIP here.

Over the last few years, Gummy has had little patches of early skin cancer removed from her cheeks. Today the doctor has to freeze some skin off, and Gummy isn't taking it too well. It is on the right side of her face, so he has her put her right hand on her left arm and press her fingers against it the whole time.

It works!

Until shot time.

After all her shouting dies down, the doctor and nurse apologize.

I'm sorry! I'm sorry!

Yeah, right. You don't look sorry.

It's so much like when a parent takes a kid to the doctor. Only in this case, the kid is a mature adult with zero verbal filters. Gummy talks them out of the next shot because she doesn't like shots. It cracks me up. I promise her a sticker and forget. Gummy and I long ago decided there is zero reason adults shouldn't get stickers.

MUCH LIKE A parent with a child, I have to entertain Gummy at her doctor's appointment. They do not race through her visit. This one takes almost two hours. She picks on me for my foot size, and I mention she gained four more pounds this week, which is a lot for someone with little elf feet. She seems kind of proud of it, although she was wearing a sweatshirt, jeans, jacket, and shoes when they weighed her.

If she'd ever struggled with her weight, she'd know it is socially acceptable to get near naked when being weighed at the doctor, even if it has to happen in the hallway.

Gummy fairs well on her memory test. Orientation is what mixes her up. She always thinks she's in her hometown or nearby. She also has no idea what time of the year it is, or which year out of the many she has lived we're in. Dates have never been my strong suit either. If you write and travel and don't pay attention to time much, it's a problem. About half the time Gummy can guess the season correctly. I usually know that one. Usually.

Some people with dementia or Alzheimer's have trouble identifying objects or how they're used, or following directions. Gummy aces those. But today she was at Burger King again. She's fused to that story. She tells everyone how Burger King now serves breakfast to the elderly, and how they eat *so much* she worries they'll eat the bottom right out of the table.

At least they all like the food at assisted living.

When she passes the sign at the entrance to her new home, she reads it out loud.

That's what they call Burger King now.

See how tenacious it is? It is that real for her. If someone says *you're not at Burger King,* it frightens her. It sends her into a free fall as surely as it would us if we were suddenly told our reality isn't as we perceive it.

It's hard not to correct her, but at this point that's the meanest thing to do to her. Isn't that weird? Dementia makes no sense, and neither does dealing with it.

WHENEVER THE NAME of Gummy's assisted living shows up on my caller ID, my mind races.

Answer the phone.

Be patient.

Go with the flow.

Sometimes it's a nurse. Usually not. Always Gummy's voice is shaky. She's upset, confused, scared. Sometimes angry. When I hear her, the patience comes, like it does when speaking with little kids. Most of the time.

Most of the time she recognizes my hello. That's gold. I love when she says in a strong voice, *Saffi.* I dread when that's gone. I'm sure it helps that she has a list of phone numbers by her bed with our names next to them.

Still.

Today she needs to get change for the store. For many years she ran a Mom and Pop type of store. I guess we can call it a Gummy and Poppy store. One of her jobs was to get to the bank in the evenings and make sure they had enough change for the next day. She is calling me for a ride to the bank to get that change, and she *must* get there tonight. Otherwise they could run out.

It seems she's gone back in time to before me, and she wants Juan to take her.

He knows I need to get that tonight. We open early.

Today I have a good excuse. I love when it's all true and I can insert some fact in there.

147

Juan went to the cabin to winterize it. There's a hard frost there tonight.

He already left?

Yeah. He won't be home until late.

That's a long drive. The bank will be closed.

The cabin is something Gummy still understands and knows from the past. At least there are still absolutes in her world. Frozen pipes at the cabin take precedence over her need to get to the bank tonight.

What are you doing?

Working. I have to write another chapter tonight.

She accepts that, which is good. It's the truth too.

I'll come pick you up at eight-thirty in the morning tomorrow.

She won't remember, but for a second it helps. I'm picking her up for a doctor's appointment, but I don't add that.

I guess that will have to do. Someone will have to stay in the store while we run to the bank.

That'll work. I'll see you in the morning.

Well, okay. I'm going to have to sleep here at Burger King tonight then. It's okay though, since it's already snowing up at the cabin.

Somehow we ended up back at Burger King, but I guess she's all right with that as long as she gets to leave there in the morning.

Leaving. Wherever her mind goes, the goal is leaving. Tonight she calmed down because I gave the illusion of helping her leave in the morning.

Maybe it's wrong to offer it. She'll never escape. She'll never get back to that illusive home she longs for. The place where things made sense. That place hasn't existed since her memory went from forgetful to forgetting she forgets.

AT 10:20 P.M. Gummy calls again.

> Saffi? I guess I'm going to need a ride home from Burger King tonight.

It is really tough to come up with a reasonable reply to that, no matter how many times it's happened now. I now have to convince her to curl up in a bed she thinks is unfamiliar, in a room she doesn't understand is hers, and go to sleep. And I can't say *for the love of all that is holy don't start packing your room!*

> *Are you in that room with the bed in it?*

> Yes.

> *You're going to need to sleep there tonight.*

> Why?

> *Because it's late and dark out.*

> Well, I know that. This place is closing and I need a ride home, or I'll have to walk.

> *Don't walk home. It's too far. Just sleep there tonight.*

> That doesn't make any sense.

> *I know, Gummy, but you have to sleep there tonight.*

> You're not making any sense. Goodbye.

WE'RE CONVINCED THE Steelers won because Gummy never lost her focus. The effort exhausted her.

149

Juan and the kids took Gummy to Buffalo Wild Wings to watch the game today. She *loves* the Steelers.

On the days they do football, I stay home and write. Just like when I first met her, I never try to fake enthusiasm for sports. Some things never change. I do wear matching socks now though. Mostly.

We never know how outings will work out. Yesterday a couple of us took her to dinner at Red Lobster, and Gummy ate *all the food*. We didn't want to draw attention to it and make her self-conscious, but we all exchanged satisfied, covert looks. She snarfed her way through appetizers, cheesy biscuits, salad, and a gigantic platter of fried everything, not to mention several sodas. Today she did the same watching the football game. We were pretty thrilled to see her eating, and kind of impressed too. It doesn't seem possible to put that much into her at any one time.

It feels good after all the times we realize too late that at her house she'd taken to often eating those horrible ninety-nine cent grocery store cakes.

Gummy enjoyed both events. This time. Sometimes she is too confused and worried to relax. It's a crap shoot, Russian roulette, a risky grab bag of ideas every time we decide to go out. No formula can ever be counted on twice. I never know who I'm going to get when I go get her.

An aide told me that when Gummy crawled into bed the other night, she remembered her granddaughter had taken her to dinner. She cried because she'd forgotten.

> How could I have forgotten that? My granddaughter took
> me to dinner!

The aide reassured her that it was okay, and she fell asleep.

It thrilled me that she'd remembered at all, while simultaneously breaking my heart for her pain and self-recrimination.

AFTER THE FOOTBALL game, I swing by to take Gummy back to assisted living. I walk her to her room and find her TV remote—in a tote bag, bottom of the closet, beneath the days of the week socks which I bought last week and were a supreme fail—and go get her a ginger ale.

You don't have to come every day.

Gummy, I don't come every day, but I like to see you.

I know you have things to do. I don't want to put that on you.

Maybe the football game helped her focus, because tonight she knows she is a grandmother, and mother, and mother-in-law, and is worried about everyone else like moms do. Maybe it is the barometric pressure, or maybe the war going on inside her head slowed for a moment. But for that moment, she remembered that she forgets. Her world made sense for hours in a row. She enjoyed family *and* football. Maybe she'll have forgotten by the time I walk to the parking lot, but today those things happened.

HOW ON GOD'S green earth can I have traveled a thousand miles north to find Gummy's house is hotter than Texas?

The guys have gone off to do whatever manly things they do this time of year that will result in the annihilation of some woodland creature. I'm staying at Gummy's house with her. We're weeding the flowerbeds. It's hot. It's boring. The only thing that keeps me going is the funky little bits of defunct yard art buried deep inside the bushes. There's a frog house in here, and ancient gnomes. I don't know why that makes it better but it does.

My job isn't to pull weeds. It's actually to take rocks out from between whatever kind of plants these are—something with greenish yellow leaves and tall stems that produce purple flowers for a short period of time. The rest of the time they look like a dead landscaping eyesore. I toss rocks into a heap on the sloped driveway. Most of them roll downhill. I suck at this, but I'm having trouble caring.

Saffi?

I turn toward Gummy's voice at the same time my hand whips a rock. I swear my brain has a serious disconnect and delay from the rest of my body. That's my excuse and I'm sticking to it. Human malfunction. What else can you say when you whip a rock at your mother-in-law? It hits her squarely in the shin.

Ow! You did that on purpose!

Gummy! I'm so sorry! I honestly didn't mean to!

She's laughing.

Yes, you did! You threw that right at me.

I wasn't thinking.

You'd better start running because I fight back.

Running would mean losing face, but since I doubt she's kidding I take that opportunity for a bathroom break. There's a dog in the kennel in the backyard. He's been making pained noises for four hours now. The sound is a cross between a howl, a bark, and a tail being stepped on. Gummy explained earlier that he likes to hunt and saw the guys leaving without him. I don't understand hunting dogs. My experience with dogs is fun and fuzzy and cozied up on the couch with me. Gummy and Poppy don't believe in dogs living indoors. They believe in working dogs. Sometimes I feel like I've married into an alien species.

During our move from New England to Texas, Juan and I stopped here. In celebration of moving to a state where we could possibly afford to buy a house with a yard, Juan gave me a puppy. We showed up at Gummy and Poppy's house in the middle of the night wearing cowboy hats and with a puppy in tow.

The time didn't matter because Poppy sat at the kitchen table sorting through paperwork for the Rod and Gun Club. I don't know what that is, but I know it involves a lot of paperwork for Poppy. Gummy perched on the couch sorting piles of cash for her job as church treasurer. They both jumped up and offered to cook despite the late hour.

Their dog lived outside in a kennel, but they allowed our dog into the house. In celebration the first thing he did was cop a squat on Gummy's new carpet—she had outgrown the peach color at last. Despite the surprise carpet-warming gift, they welcomed my carsick, squatting puppy and never said a rude word about it. They insisted we sleep in their room, because it had the most comfortable bed. Elaborate meals were cooked from scratch, ice-cream and cakes were stocked in all varieties. Dirty dishes vanished before you could take them to the kitchen yourself. Every morning eggs and bacon were cooked, and Poppy added extra salt to the bacon. It gave me a part-time vegetarian heart attack, but I'm sorry to say I accepted my share and sneaked some to my squatty puppy.

Tonight Gummy and I are going to see a play with her sisters. She shows me ceramic projects they've been painting with her. A local shop offered her a job painting things they sell. She's thinking about taking it.

What do you like best?

The Santa Clauses.

The glazed white and gold ones?

No. The Currier and Ives old-fashioned ones.

You would like those. They take forever. How about I paint you one every year?

Really? I'd love that.

We go outside to feed the fish in her koi pond while waiting for our ride to the theater.

What's that one's name?

I don't name them anymore.

Why? Juan said you always name them!

We got acid rain and they all died in one night. I cried for a week. Poppy thought I lost my mind. These are new fish, and I'm not naming them anymore.

That's so sad, Gummy.

See that frog? I got him when I visited you in Boston.

From where?

I don't know. Poppy and I stopped somewhere and I saw him and took him. I brought him home in a McDonald's cup. He wouldn't fit in a cup now.

Yeah. I think you'd need a car seat.

Speaking of car seats, when are you going to make me a grandbaby?

How about we just name the frog Juan Junior?

I joke, but I hate when she brings up kids. Juan and I've been married years now and it's just not happening. She brings it up a lot. Everyone does.

chapter eighteen

GUMMY BONES

Gummy has always had a great sense of humor. Today her funny bone is getting tickled as she's quizzing me about *why can she not remember* taking medicine and going to the doctor.

Why can't I go home?

Because you need to take medicine.

Why can't I take it at home?

Because you can't remember to take it.

When are they going to give me the medicine?

The doctors started you on it a couple months ago.

I don't remember that. Are you sure?

Yes. The doctors have been treating you since late summer.

WHAT ARE THEY TREATING ME FOR THAT I CAN'T REMEMBER?

Your memory.

She laughs and laughs, dropping flat on her bed to hold her stomach.

That's kind of funny. You've got to admit, that's kind
of funny.

It is, Gummy, kind of.

This is what we have in common—besides her son. Inappropriate
humor. Sometimes it is funny, except when it's not.

THE AIDES WON'T let Gummy out of the memory care unit by herself, so she calls the police on them.

The calls from her room go through a switchboard. Switchboard
operators are the ones who could write a book. They hear it all. Suffice
to say when you ask the switchboard at assisted living to call the police
because you're being held hostage by the nurses who work at Burger King,
you lose credibility.

The staff never take it personally, and they respond with kindness. It's
interesting that Gummy's only complaint with assisted living—aka Burger
King—is that they won't let her go home. Mostly she loves those ladies,
except those brief moments when she hates them of course.

It's kind of like marriage that way.

Since Gummy usually thinks she knows the staff from Burger King,
she teases them. She likes to call them hussies, and give them a little slap
on the backside.

Sometimes I wonder if this is something she did at Burger King.

I'm thinking not, but you've got to wonder.

Juan and I often exchange ideas on what works and what doesn't with
both the staff and family members. There are times when someone will tell
Gummy exactly where she is, and argue the Burger King scenario. You always
have to take a wild guess how that's going to go over. It can end in tears and
acceptance, or frustration and anger. But it *always* ends up being erased,
and reset to what makes sense for Gummy.

That's the Burger King reboot.

At least that's been the case for a couple months.

We have to roll with it. Anything else is just us trying to make ourselves feel better, and trying to force logic into Wonderland.

Wonderland repels logic.

THERE WAS THAT time in P-town. We were living outside of Boston and Gummy took the ferry over without a clue what she was getting herself into. I remember her holding up a pair of crotchless panties, insisting it was the top to a thong. You've got to give it to her. Upside down it could work, if you're Gummy-sized.

After Gummy's Provincetown education, we all went out for lunch somewhere on the Cape. Listening to Gummy and Poppy with their southern accent ordering from a waiter with his South Boston accent made life worth living.

Or that time in Texas when Gummy decided to make stuffed jalapenos. I ran to the store to pick up the peppers, and came back with what looked like, but may or may not have been, jalapenos. She cut and sliced them like anyone from the northeast might have, with no rubber gloves and an occasional swipe or two across the nose and at least one eye rub.

All hell broke loose then. Her eyes swelled shut, and she laughed herself to tears. I ran to get a washcloth and Juan ran to get his camera. It kind of runs in their family. Gummy never made stuffed jalapenos again. She still laughs about that story, when someone tells it to her.

TONIGHT I AM making my sour cream chicken enchiladas, a recipe I made up years ago. The prep takes far too long, and they're made with so many unhealthy ingredients I've tried to wipe it from my family's mind for years. One of my kids requests it every birthday. Mostly I offer to take them out for their birthdays, but there's always that one lone kid trying to force me to be domestic or maternal. Gummy is sharking around the house moving things. I did as much as I could before I picked her up from assisted living.

The table is set. At least it was until Gummy headed in there. I'm making rice, one of the things I couldn't prep until the last minute.

She wanders up to me with a book in her hands.

Did you write this?

Yes.

It has your name on it.

Yes.

You wrote a book called *Bitch Witch*?

Yes.

I will slap your ass.

I laugh and she wanders back out. When I peek into the dining room she's filling her purse with matching *Bitch Witch* bookmarks. It must not have bothered her too much. She scrapes the last of them from the bookcase and crams them in too. Ah, well. It's not like I'm going to have time for a book signing anyway.

All the enchiladas get eaten. That's a first. I made them in a pan that barely fits into the oven. If I ever was going to get domestic, I'd want a professional size oven. Years ago Gummy, who's never enjoyed cooking either, told me to cook a lot if you're going to be forced to cook at all, that way you can freeze and reheat it. She said if you're going to put in all that effort, it's just as easy to double or triple a recipe. Then you won't have to do it again anytime soon.

I took that bit of brilliant advice to heart.

For all the good it did me this time.

We have a store bought ice-cream cake. Gummy went with me when I picked it up. She insisted she'd wait in the car. When I walked out of the store approximately three minutes later, she was wandering around the parking lot with my car alarm going off. She forgot where I was. Waiting in the car is off the list forevermore.

Where'd you go?

I ran in the store. Where'd you go?

I was looking for you.

I had to pick up the birthday cake.

I can't have cake. I'm getting fat.

You're fine! Get in the car before the cake melts. It's ice-cream.

I can't have ice-cream. I look pregnant. Look at my stomach.

I help her into the Jeep.

Is there something you'd like to tell me? How'd you get that pregnant stomach?

He's way younger than me, and rich.

Gummy!

I'm laughing and she's grinning.

Don't act like that couldn't be true. I've still got it.

INSTEAD OF TRADITIONAL candles I bought those number kind. I got the wrong ones. I'm off a year. For my own kid. This thrills Gummy more than anything has had the power to do in a long time.

You forget too.

I sure do, Gummy.

You always did.

Thanks a lot.

There's no point in arguing that while I may be one to lose track of time, or leave an umbrella behind, I almost never forget a story and could probably recite every one that she's ever told me.

To atone for my math error I tape a piece of paper with the correct number over the candle. My kid isn't buying it. This will go down in family legend. I hate getting a starring role in those stories. Gummy sidles around the table when we start to sing. None of us can sing except her. We stop and listen. It's the best present that kid will get. She eats a huge piece of cake. We sit around the table and tell stories.

> Remember when we used to visit Gummy and Poppy, and Poppy would take us to the store and buy us all the ice cream we wanted?
>
> Remember when we used to play band with Gummy and Poppy? We'd march around the house with instruments and Poppy would sing all the wrong lyrics.
>
> Remember when we played baseball together at the cabin? Mom guarded second base and Gummy ran to her, grabbed her boobs, and shouted *Second base! Second base! I got to second base!*
>
> Remember playing Bingo outside in the rain at the family reunion?
>
> Remember when Gummy taught us to eat Cheetos with forks?

It goes on and on, and Gummy sits quietly and listens, grinning. I drive her back to assisted living late that evening.

This is the best day. This is the best day I think I've ever had.

chapter nineteen

CRANKY PANTS

Right now I'm very angry at Gummy. The last couple days have been very bad no good terrible days in her world.

She's been calling the police on the memory care nurses because they won't let her walk home. Trying to call, anyway. Since she goes through the switchboard and opens with the fact that the nurses at Burger King won't let her walk to another state in the dark, it once more doesn't go the way she plans. Still. She is spending a lot of time threatening and trying.

Their crimes, you ask?

> They said I'm staying here now.
>
> Some of my pillows are missing.
>
> They keep trying to take my clothes after I wear them. I have to hide them.
>
> I can't find my remote.

Every time I've taken her out this week, she fusses that I don't give her any notice and she always looks like a hobo.

> Nobody told me!

161

I called you earlier and told you.

What are you talking about? Nobody called me.

Lately her memory is spectacularly poor. It's like holding sand in your fist under water at the beach, only I don't think Gummy can make a fist anymore. Everything rolls into oblivion.

Today I make a point of calling her several times to give her the NASA countdown on how many minutes she has to make herself beautiful before I come for her.

I'm good enough to get out of here. I quit this place!

She is mad when I arrive, only partly because she looks like a hobo. I realize I can't win a battle of the wits against dementia, but I am tenacious enough to try.

Sorry, did I say tenacious? I meant stupid.

The plan is to get her a manicure, which she isn't happy about either.

A manicure is the least of my problems!

This is true. But her nails look like one of those witches in *Hocus Pocus*, and when she loses it and goes after one of the nurses she scratches them up. Since there's about nothing I can do to fix dementia, I focus on things I can control. Like keeping Gummy tidy and somewhat happy. At least when she looks at her hands she can feel some pride in the fact that they look nice.

I take her to have her nails cut and shaped into a less lethal and beautiful gel manicure. She tolerates it. It takes a long time and a lot of patience on the part of the manicurist. Gummy forgets what is happening and scratches or fidgets, messing up the polish before it can dry.

My grand plan is to take her to dinner after, but she is so out of it I decide to take her back to assisted living to eat. It's like trying to communicate with a sleepwalker.

Per usual she doesn't know where she is when we return, and I walk her down the hall to her room with the intention of getting her situated.

Oh, this is Burger King and this is my locker down here.

I guess that's as good as it gets.

It's when I walk into her room that I become angry. It's trashed, with garbage and shards of ceramics scattered everywhere. Obviously she has had some kind of temper tantrum. I can't say how much time either the aides or I have spent in here trying to make order. This time it's worse than usual. Her coffee table is against the wall with a stack of pillows on top. She must have climbed on top of it to reach the shelf by her ceiling to take down her treasures.

That shelf is the only decoration left in the room. We thought it was safe because it seemed impossible to reach. It looks like she stood on top of pillows, on top of the coffee table, and used another pillow to smack at the things and knock them down. Everything is broken. A ceramic Bible, a Native American statue she had painted ages ago, and a couple teapots.

Once before I felt like spanking her, and this time it takes everything I have not to yell. I save it though, because it wouldn't penetrate tonight. Instead I clean up the mess, give her a hug, and leave.

Even now I'm still angry with her. If she was anybody else I think I would call this feeling the last straw. But she's not anybody else. She has dementia and nothing I say or do is going to change that. Despite that I start formulating a lecture in my mind. Sometimes it's tough to always have to be the adult. I don't want to take the high road. This has got to stop.

Dementia or not, we are going to have a chat. If the caseworker had seen that, or the psychiatrist, her world might have gotten a whole lot smaller today. I'm at least a bit terrified maybe it needs to.

EARLIER TODAY ONE of my kids took Gummy to watch the Steelers game. He gave glowing updates on how she behaved. She remembered where she was staying and why, and that she was going to have to go back there after the game. But like an elderly version of Cinderella, all good things must end. At four o'clock, which in the winter is prime sundowning time, she vanished.

A few hours later my landline rings. I keep it for emergencies and Gummy. Here in the bogs of the shire, mobile phones work when they feel like it, and don't when the wind blows hard or the planets don't align properly.

> Hey, Saffi. I just wanted to let you know that I'm at Burger King and the people here say the doctor says I have to stay here. I have a memory problem and they said if I stay here and don't do anything and rest it'll get better. So I don't like it, but I'm going to listen to them. They give me a pill—a big one and a little one. And that's all I can have to eat. Well, I can have other things to eat but I'm going to try to take those pills and get better.

She tries to give me her phone number, but can't remember it. I assure her I have it.

She asks me to take care of her husband for her, then considers this and asks if he is alive. Many tears follow. Most of them are hers. Sadly I'm getting used to it.

Gummy had a lot of good in her weekend. She had a lot of fun too. I never have words with her over her temper tantrum. I realize there is no point. If anybody deserves a temper tantrum, it's somebody with dementia or Alzheimer's.

AFTER *THE INCIDENT* the other day, with Gummy literally climbing the walls and throwing stuff around, I decide to take the weekend off. She got out and about all weekend with other family, and I talk to her on the phone. It feels good to catch up on house things, work, and recharge my Gummy batteries.

Last night I stayed up until four-thirty in the morning writing, so today I decide not to visit either. Oddly enough I don't hear from her until later. She's forgotten about agreeing to stay at assisted living by then, and is back to being stuck at Burger King and looking for a ride home.

I have just run a hot bath and lit a candle, set my iPod to the right mood music, and found the bath salts. This is all prep for another late night write. You've got to ease into some things in life. The phone rings.

Gummy is trying to call her husband to come get her and can't figure out why he isn't picking up the phone tonight. Her stomach hurts. Badly. Where is everyone? She sounds so lost. We talk for a few minutes and after we hang up I consider going to visit.

On a whim I called the main nurse on duty instead. This time of night the nurses are all earning their way into heaven. It's sundowner madness. You've got the runners trying to escape, tearful residents who want to go the heck home asking questions, arguments, the occasional accusations of theft, lost glasses, missing remotes and socks, water seeping from under the door of someone who's left their bath running, the guy who clucks like a chicken dancing up and down the hall, etc. etc. etc.

I don't understand why this entire premise isn't a sitcom, because it's laughter through tears a good deal of the time.

A panting nurse answers the phone. I can only assume she's been chasing a runner. I appreciate that any time of day I call, they take the time to listen and respond. We discuss Gummy's medication. I am worried that her new stomach medicine isn't being administered, and that the doctor's take on why Gummy's stomach always hurts isn't the problem. I am worried about her being in her room, lonely and sad. I am worried that she can't go three days without the Gummy Whisperer.

The nurse reassures me that she is indeed getting her medicine. That she agrees with the doctor on the source of the problem—not eating enough except when she is with us, chronic anxiety, and stress. She gives me the low-down on every fun thing Gummy did today and tells me what she is going to give her for her stomach.

Sometimes those nurses and aides end up reassuring the family too. Lord, I'm glad they're there.

All hail memory care workers.

So I got my bath.

All hail baths.

And now I shall stop worrying and write.

All hail night writes.

Maybe not that last thing, but it sure is my happy place, and it feels good to escape the real world, even if I spend the entire night writing about it.

WHEN I ARRIVE in the memory care unit, I overhear people talking about someone being expelled. What they're actually saying is that someone is going to have to go out of here tonight. I didn't even know that happened. There's a lot of staff hurrying through the doors, so I know something is going down, and I'm pretty anxious as I go in.

Fortunately it doesn't look like it's Gummy causing the trouble. She's sitting in the front area at a table with one of her comrades, having a snack, and likely waiting for a ride home. Thank God!

All the aides and nurses are preoccupied with a woman in the midst of a third degree meltdown. I'm not sure what that woman's issues are. It looks like more than dementia or Alzheimer's, but what do I know?

I sit at the table with Gummy and her friend, but they hardly pay me any mind.

The lady causing the commotion keeps slamming her door open and shut and screaming at the top of her lungs about her pants. Every time she hurls a new complaint, Gummy and her girlfriend offer a sensible response.

It's darkly humorous.

I WANT MY PAAAAAAANTS!

You just had them and took them off.

166

I NEED MY PAAAAAAANTS!

Yes, you do, and you should keep them on.

PANTS PANTS PAAAAAAAANTS!!!!!!!

They should fire her.

That last came out of Gummy because she's back at Burger King tonight. In the course of a few minutes, between Gummy and her friend, they spill two drinks and drop a snack. It's then I notice Gummy's hands are shaking.

Despite their snarky responses, they're both a bit upset by the commotion.

It takes me some time to convince them both to come down the hall to the lounge area with me.

Let's go work on a puzzle.

After repeating it several times and helping them relocate by carrying Gummy's purse and moving at a walker pace for her friend, I manage to get them to move.

I think an ambulance may have taken the pants lady away, but we're now busy working a dang three-hundred piece diva kitten puzzle that I've done half a dozen times now—and it *never* gets any easier. Both Gummy and her girlfriend are way better at it. Showoffs.

Gummy enjoys a black cat cookie I brought, and seems rather impressed that I made it. Black cat cookies are made with chocolate cake mix, peanut butter, and candy corn eyes. I even added a wooden stick with a bow on it. They're homemade. From scratch. Gummy's not the only one impressed. I am too. I haven't made them in years. I did it for Gummy. I kept thinking I shouldn't put anything off until next year. I don't want to think about next year, or the fact that Gummy might not notice cookie details by then. Her girlfriend is diabetic and can't have one of the extras I brought, so Gummy thoughtfully turns her back every time she takes a bite.

Before I leave we sit in her room and talk for a bit. I run her bath and fill it with her favorite bath salts.

I want to go home.

I know you do, Gummy, but you can't tonight.

I can walk if you can't take me.

No, don't walk. It's dark. Stay here tonight.

I don't want to be here alone.

You're not going to be alone.

Will you stay?

I can stay for a while. How about you take a bath while the water is hot?

I'm afraid to take a bath.

Why?

I've been thinking what if I fall asleep and my head goes under the water?

I'll stay here and wake you up if that happens.

Okay.

Tonight Gummy really wants to go home. Not in the usual angry or confused way, but far more desperate. Far more *I've got to get out of this place.* I'm thankful she'll forget this. Worrying about drowning is new. I'm not sure what to make of it.

She manages that bath in less time than a little boy during summer vacation. I wonder if she actually got in the tub, and kiss her goodnight. This is the first time I really don't want to leave her alone, so I'm looking forward to tomorrow morning when she has reset to a fresh new day.

Hopefully I can do that too.

NOT LONG AFTER Juan and I married, we went for a weekend visit to Gummy and Poppy's to pick up our wedding photos. Since we got married in Juan's hometown, that's where the photographer lived. Gummy had already picked up the photos for us and chosen her favorites for the album. Since she did her usual stellar job, and put quite a bit of thought into it, I kept my grumbling to a minimum and mostly to myself.

From her attic she dragged out a box of old photos so I could see her wedding pictures.

> *You looked fourteen years old!*
>
> I was not! I was nineteen!

We look through piles of Gummy's wedding pictures. I don't point out that nineteen isn't much older than fourteen, but I'm thinking it. She knows I'm thinking it. Women can read each other too well. I switch tactics. Fortunately I genuinely think her wedding dress is spectacular.

> *Your dress is flawless. I think that's the most beautiful wedding dress I've ever seen.*
>
> That was the style then. Would you like one of the pictures?
>
> *I would love one!*
>
> Just promise me if you divorce my son that you'll give it back.

I don't take the photo she's offering me. I can't believe she said that. It isn't the first time something like that has come out of her mouth. There's no basis for the comments. Later I angrily mention it to Juan. He logically points out that several people who live in Gummy's hometown have divorced lately.

> It's on her mind.
>
> *She doesn't like me.*
>
> If my mom didn't like you, you'd know it.

Her hair is pretty dark.

It's black! Isn't that hysterical?

Gummy is holding my newborn in the recovery room at the hospital, trying to smooth four inches of fuzzy hair down. It doesn't work.

Everyone else in the family is blond.

I know! If I hadn't seen her come out, I wouldn't have believed she's mine!

You're blond, and so is Juan and your son. Poppy is a red-head though.

That's not red. That's coal black.

Now, you were at your high school reunion last summer.

Wasn't that around nine months ago?

What?

It took me a while to replay that conversation in my head and under-stand the implication. I was still on a newborn baby high. Even after the baby's roots grew in red, and then turned blond with calico tips, I was still mad at Gummy for that remark.

BEFORE CALLER ID, one had to hope for the best when their phone rang. Sometimes it was your mother-in-law.

How's my grandbaby?

Sleeping. Thank God. It's been a loud day.

How's Juan?

He's not here. He went on his archery trip to the Grand Canyon with his college friends.

What? He left you alone in Texas with a newborn baby?

Yes. He said that my pregnancy had been rough on him. Gummy didn't respond.

Gummy? Are you there?

You didn't kill him?

Oh, I thought about it.

I'd have done more than think about it.

That's not true. Juan got his outdoorsman gene from Poppy. Gummy often tells me that she loves hunting season, because the guys are out of her hair and she does everything her way while they're gone. I appreciate her support just the same.

The only reason I didn't was I figured I've have to clean up the mess.

That's true. You probably would have. I can't believe he left you there alone with a new baby. I'll come visit.

I'm pretty sure Poppy was off hunting or fishing at the birth of every one of his kids. But since Gummy didn't live within driving distance, she always worried about us being alone. No matter the population of the state or the friend network, we were alone without her.

He invited me to come with him.

Are you kidding? And you didn't jump on that?

Right? It's so tempting to go camping with a newborn and Juan's college friends.

You could kill him when he gets back.

I'll probably settle for making him regret the day he was born.

That's good too. I do that to Poppy all the time. He says I'm good at it. Do you want some pointers?

chapter twenty
THE SONG THAT NEVER ENDS

Remember the woman who got taken away last night? Today she is at the table across from Gummy as I walk into the memory care unit.

Gummy sits serenely next to two gentlemen, offering sassy answers when one of them tries to strike up conversation with me.

Where are you from?

Stop talking to my company.

I just want to know where she's from.

She doesn't want to talk to you. She's here to talk to me.

But I just want to know where she's from.

Why? You're too old for her.

Clearing my throat in my best *I'm right here* way does no good. This isn't about me. This is their conversation. A moment later he persists, asking again where I'm from. I cut Gummy off.

I'm from here.

Hopefully that'll fit into wherever he thinks he is. He shakes his head.

You're from Iowa.

What? I don't think I've ever even been to Iowa to fake it. I don't respond.

Des Moines, Iowa.

I keep my mouth shut as he starts talking about Iowa.

She writes books!

Hey! Gummy remembered I write, and she told someone! I look at her in surprise and she grins. Maybe a title like *Bitch Witch* is some sort of mnemonic pattern or memory aid for daughter-in-law. It's the only book that sticks in her head. She does still have all those bookmarks that she swiped.

I want to read her books. Why doesn't she have her books?

Why are you still talking to my company?

Gummy is annoyed with him, but he barely notices she's talking. It hits me then that this isn't really a conversation between them. It's them conversing with themselves. They're only crossing paths in the most happenstance way. He's still going on about Iowa, and Gummy is glaring.

The gentleman on her other side wants someone to guess his age.

Memory care is like one of those chapter-a-day stories on Wattpad or in the newspaper. You have to wait till tomorrow to see what happens, and while you're waiting the editor gets in there and mixes everything up. So good luck following or figuring it out, and try not to expect a linear pattern of any sort.

Gummy and I go outside to enjoy some fresh air. We sit on a bench in the sun and chat, and I ask her about the woman who'd been taken away last night. She remembers.

Can you believe she's back?

You're kidding! After all that, I am surprised.

They need to fire her. I would but I'm not her supervisor.

I don't suppose I need to mention that we are at Burger King again.

> Thanks for coming to see me. I haven't seen you in a long time.

> *It's not that long.*

> What are you talking about? I can't remember the last time I saw you.

> *Are you saying I'm easy to forget?*

> My memory is crap. I need to get out of here. I've been trying to call Poppy to come get me. He never answers the phone, so I don't even know if he knows where I am.

> *Er. Oh.*

> Do you know where he's at? Did we get divorced or something?

I stare at her, deer-in-headlights fashion.

> Oh, my God! I forgot! I remember now. How long ago did he die?

> *Eight years.*

> That long? That's how my memory is now. I'm forgetting everything.

It seems to be less traumatic when *she* remembers, versus us reminding her.

> *Not everything. You remembered that by yourself. That's pretty good.*

> If you say so. I need to get myself together. I need to quit this place, and get my house straightened out. This is my last day.

The sun sinks lower in the sky and the air turns cold, so we walk through the courtyard and back inside.

You know your way around here better than I do!

I come here a lot.

You do? What do you come here for?

I'm stalking you.

Oh, I have that problem everywhere I go! No one could blame you.

Do you want to take the stairs up?

Are we going upstairs? I didn't know there were stairs here. I have to pay attention so I know how to get around this place. I don't know where my head is at.

It takes longer than you'd imagine getting back to Gummy's room. She manages the stairs fine. The problem is she wanders off in the wrong direction or gets distracted.

Nope, Gummy, we're going to go left here.

You know this place better than I do! Look at that picture. Isn't that nice? I see that picture everywhere I go lately. Have you noticed that?

I think I've only seen it here. It's nice. Go left here too.

In her room we find all of her clothes neatly folded into piles on her bed. All of them. She's packing to leave again.

How about I move these to the couch so they won't be in your way?

That's where they were! I put them on my bed until I find my suitcase.

You know it's dinner time.

What are you talking about?

They're going to have dinner down the hall in a few minutes.

How do you know that?

I saw them getting it ready when we came in.

I don't have any money.

You don't need any money.

What are you talking about? They're not going to give me dinner for free.

Yes, here they do. Juan set it all up, I think.

If you add *I think* to a lie, it lessens the degree of severity. I'm pretty sure that's a thing even though I just invented it.

Why's Juan paying for this?

Because you're his favorite mother.

It's getting pretty deep in here.

I leave Gummy waiting in the dining room for her prepaid dinner, with plans to watch all the breaking news after. If she forgets to do that, it'll probably be the best thing she forgot all day.

GUMMY COMES FROM a large, tight-knit family who always make an effort to get together. She's used to going to football games and plays or spending time with grandkids, her sisters and their families—until she stopped remembering to go.

Today is Juan's birthday. Tonight he's just returning home from a trip. Our family is gathered for dinner and pie. Everyone sits around the table talking, telling stories and laughing again. At this time we become Gummy's memory for the moments she has forgotten. If there is family therapy for people with dementia, this would certainly be one of the best kinds.

At least it is with Gummy's disposition, and at this stage of the disease. I'm certainly no expert. I'm pointing that out, in case you haven't noticed how much I'm winging it from moment to moment. You never know if things are going to work. Today it works. So today is perfect.

And Gummy is in a really good mood today.

During the drive to my house, she enthuses over how beautiful it is in the shire this time of year. This fall is spectacular. If you don't live where trees change colors, you might not realize that every year it's different.

Some years the leaves turn gold and brown and fall off. Some years if the weather is bad, the leaves don't last long at all. One good storm and they can all come down before the season has time to reach its full potential. This year we're having beautiful weather, and so many of the trees are various shades of red—crimson, scarlet, burgundy—mixed with all the yellows, oranges, and golds. It's spectacular, especially in clear sunlight with the bluest of skies.

On the way back to assisted living we drive in rainy darkness, with autumn leaves drifting down around us. Some land on the windshield before being wiped away. Gummy gushes about how much fun she had.

> That was a good time.
>
> *I had fun too.*
>
> They made me laugh.
>
> *Me too.*

Back at memory care, Gummy leads the way straight to her room.

This is where I am now. This is everything.

She opens her closet to show me her small clothing collection. Today she remembers she belongs here.

This is the kind of day we all wish for when we think about what family time can be. You know the way it never really is, except maybe once or twice? The feeling is fleeting. It's too bad Gummy won't remember today because she has had a wonderful time.

AFTER OUR FIRST Griswold Family Vacation Thanksgiving together, shortly after our marriage, I planned never to have another with my in-laws or quite possibly with my husband. We'd driven through a few states after work on Wednesday, arrived late, crashed into bed, and now sat around Gummy's resplendent dining room table, searching for something to talk about.

The new mother-in-law went with Juan's old girlfriend.

Guess who I saw in town the other day?

Who, Mom?

Your ex-fiancé! She looks great.

Mom! Please don't bring her up again. Saffi bitches about it all the way back to Boston!

The room went still. Except for the part where I kicked a dent into Juan's shin under the table.

What?

Nothing, honey.

Why did you kick me?

Because you, my dear, are an ass. And a colossally dumb one at that.

Only that very last line isn't true. All the rest is so accurate I could safely put quotation marks around each line. I would, except it'd mess up the pattern of the rest of the story. No joke, these things were said, except my last line. What I actually said to the *Why did you kick me?* sounded more like *Did I kick you? I don't think I kicked you.*

I've regretted my pardon ad infinitum since that day. There are times in life when you are perfectly justified in letting your thoughts fly right outta your mouth. Unfortunately I satisfied myself with feigning civility, and then bitching at him all the way back to Boston.

IT'S BEEN TWO days since Gummy called.

At least that is *almost* out of my mouth when my phone rings.

I'm taking two days a week off, in a row, to work on a book and generally get my thoughts into a semi-logical order. My kids say I'm starting to get confused like Gummy. One time I referred to the assisted living staff as "Gummy's coworkers" and suddenly everyone is a critic.

I blame it on all her comments about working at Burger King.

Wonderland is contagious.

Anyway, it's sundowning time and she needs a ride home. Speaking of logical, Juan takes the call. He tells her she can't go home until the doctors say she can. Snuggled next to him on the couch, I can hear her arguing through the phone.

What doctors? I don't see any doctors.

Yes, you do. They have you on memory pills.

What pills? I don't take any pills.

Yes, you do. The nurses give them to you a few times a day.

What nurses? I don't see any nurses.

You've heard it before.

We try to be as honest with her as possible, so she never has a reason not to trust us. Sometimes I think being honest is more important to us than her. Maybe she needs more patience than anything.

It's Saturday before I take her out again. We go to Panera for salads and leave her purse behind. Fortunately a guy working there runs after us in the parking lot and returns it. That's the shire. I take her back to her room and put it safely into her closet. The room doesn't seem familiar to her this time, and she wanders around looking at things.

There's seasonal stuff she makes in day club all over. A beach themed tote bag. An apple framed chalkboard. Today she shows me a white paper bag decorated with Halloween stickers and ribbons with a card attached. It's written in crayon, and from a little girl named Haley. She introduces herself and asks questions about what it was like when Gummy was little.

Gummy is really taken with it and opens the bag.

Inside the bag are tissues, lip balm, and candy. Gummy thinks it is sweet and is delighted with the card, reading and rereading it.

I assume a children's group or class visited. I remember taking my kids to nursing homes and such when they were in various groups. It never occurred to me until now how much those visits mean to someone in Gummy's situation.

The card and gift are brilliant, because when Gummy forgets, she'll be delighted to come across it again. She gets cards and letters from friends and her church regularly and carries them around with her. Every time she sorts through them it's new.

Sometimes she wonders why her mail is coming to Burger King. Sometimes she can't figure out why people from church are sending her cards, because it's right up the street and she'll see them Sunday. And sometimes she shows them to me and tells me about the people. I think Haley's card will make it to the save pile.

SUNDAY NIGHT JUAN and I are showing Gummy around her assisted living facility. We found her sitting in her room feeling sad, as there is nothing to do there, according to her.

This is what I do all the time. Sit here on my butt and
do nothing.

Juan pulls out his always available patience and tells her where she
is and why again. We walk up and down stairs, in and out of elevators, and
examine the nooks and crannies of each floor. Gummy gets a guided tour of
the library, the auditorium, the dining hall, and the downstairs where she
attends day club. At a bulletin board we stop and review daily entertainment
options. There are sing-alongs, day trips, exercise classes, and plays to go to.
Memory care residents don't have all the choices and freedom that those in
regular assisted living do, but they do have options.

It's seems like the problem is getting their cooperation.

Seeing all the interesting things going on around her, Gummy briefly
regains her excitement. She imagines she's managed to get back home.

This is up the street from my house, isn't it?

No, Mom. This is assisted living.

I don't know what you're talking about.

Gummy starts crying because she doesn't know where she is. I find a
tissue in my purse and give it to her. We hurry back to her room and seeing it
helps cheer her up. She recognizes it as familiar and life is good again.

This is where I'm staying now. Poppy bought this place
in case we get too much company. I don't know why I'm
staying here though.

No, Mom. This is your room at assisted liv—

I interrupt Juan's explanation. It's what I do.

It's a nice room. I like your couch. Is that bed comfortable?

Juan nods at me in complicit agreement. Sometimes it's hard to remember reality is fluid here, and rather subjective.

It's very comfortable. I'm not staying though. Can one of you drive me home?

I have a conference call I have to get back for, Mom.

We can't tonight. Juan has a phone meeting starting in twenty minutes, so we need to go. I'll see you in the morning!

This is sundowning. We're not getting anywhere. My spidey senses tell me retreat is the best option. Plus it's true that he has a call to get back for. Juan hugs Gummy and tells her goodnight. I don't think she's at all sure who we are.

Try. Fail. Try. Fail. But keep on trying, right?

BACK WHEN PEOPLE could waltz through security to meet planes at the gate, we went to visit Gummy and Poppy for another Thanksgiving. Yes. I know I swore I'd never do it again. I do that a lot. Lie to myself. I lie to myself with a wild abandon I'd never be comfortable unleashing on the general population.

I'll never eat sugar again, after this chocolate.
There's not enough time now. I'll work out tonight.
It wasn't so bad last time, and holidays are for families.
I can work full-time, and finish college, and get to the gym.

Gummy spotted me as I deplaned, raced over and yanked my coat open, eyeing my belly.

Do you have a surprise for me?

I shoot a withering look at Juan. If you're not married, you might not be aware that you're each responsible for whatever comes out of the mouths of the other's family. We'd been married a few years now, and *still* crickets in the baby department. Not that I thought I needed to start blowing out babies hours into our marriage. I'm all pro career and take time for freedom before settling into the family thing, if ever.

That's another lie I tell to myself. We've been trying to have a baby for a couple years now. Gummy's comment stings.

So do all the others over the course of the eternal holiday weekend.

What are you waiting for?

The longer you wait, the more problems you'll have.

Juan's ex is having her second! That's what I heard. I never see her, but I *heard* that.

If you would get on the ball and make a grandchild, we'd buy one of those *round* wrought iron cribs you loved at Macy's! We really would.

I try not to be bothered by the comments and fail. But I burn the last one into my memory. I really did like that insanely expensive crib, and after all the grief I'm not above cashing in on that promise when the time comes.

chapter twenty-one

BEGIN AGAIN

C alling, or waiting for the doctor to return my call concerning Gummy, has now become a regular thing. Gummy is having stomach problems and the medicine she takes is making it worse. Her little belly is swollen and hard, and makes impressive noises heard from two rooms away.

She *wants to go home* today. She's been calling me all day. She sounds as tired of asking about going home as I am of trying to formulate an answer that won't upset her.

We've all been sticking with the honest *you're in assisted living while the doctors treat your memory, and you can't go home until they say you can* response. To which she replies that she hasn't seen a doctor in ages, what the hell is everyone talking about, take her home or she's going to walk. The usual.

Today I'm wondering what the doctor's next cure for her belly will be. I don't care how bad her memory is. There are certain things that stick with a person.

I'm having visions of having to administer an intestinal tsunami or helping her through invasive testing. This is a tough situation, but I'm very aware it could always be worse.

Color me checking airline ticket miles to see how far away I can get and how quickly I can do it.

Gotta go. Get it? Funny, not funny.

GUMMY'S POOCHY BELLY has to be X-rayed tonight. It really threw her that here in the shire we do X-rays at night. I am glad that we do that because today I had a hundred things on my to-do list.

Sitting in the waiting room at the hospital, we watch a toddler with thick curly hair come running up the hall. He is fast, and his parents are walking a good distance behind him. Gummy watches him, worrying he will fall and face plant. He doesn't. She hunkers down in her seat, puts a hand up to her mouth, and stage-whispers to me.

> You go distract the parents. I'll grab him and run. Meet me
> around back with the car.

She really, really wants a baby.

After the X-ray we return to assisted living. One of the nurses asks her how the X-ray went.

> What the hell are you talking about? I didn't have an X-ray.
> You're such a pain in my ass. Why are you here? I thought
> you were working at church tonight.

I want to laugh at how she talks to people she thinks are from her church. I'm on to you staunch Methodists now. Tonight she has her full-on feisty attitude going full blast, but wants to run by the bank and get a lot of change because she is planning to open the store tomorrow and they are out.

Tonight she is time-traveling. Time is no longer linear. Gummy still remembers all sorts of things, but not in the right order. It's still easy to have a conversation with her, unless she's pestering you to take her home, or you are expecting her to hold her train of thought.

She's in her room, which she explains Poppy rented and stuck her in. I'm glad it's his fault for a change. I give her ginger ale with a straw and a pumpkin muffin with cream cheese frosting. I instruct her to put this into her poochy belly because I suspect the doctors are going to put her on a liquid diet this weekend. I leave her eating her subversive treat and happily watching FOX News—CNN apparently pissed her off and she's changed camps for probably an hour until FOX pisses her off too.

EXACTLY THIRTY-THREE TRILLION years ago today, I married Gummy's oldest son. To commemorate the occasion Gummy and I went to see the movie *Storks*.

This is the first time I tried to mix a movie in the theater with dementia. Gummy's memory doesn't let her follow a storyline well. She usually gets bored. *Storks* doesn't require viewers to follow much, and she enjoys it, and every preview before it starts. She drinks most of her Coke and munches on popcorn, and forgets about her problems for a while. Because *babies*. The storks delivered *babies*. In all the world, the number one joy bringer for Gummy is *babies*.

Gummy is one of those people it is easy to imagine as a kid. This is likely because she allows her inner kid to drive most of the time.

Watching her today I find I'm not sad for what has been, because despite everything, Gummy still has moments of absolute happiness. Despite this effing dementia, her life still has joy. She gets a kick out of watching kids trick or treat, dreaming of babies, joking with strangers, and being her extroverted self. She's quick-witted and knows how to act in social situations, and she can make people smile. In a group of strangers she's okay if she knows what to do, and nobody wounds her pride (and if all the planets in the Memory Constellation align perfectly).

Back in her room Gummy announces she's going to crochet a baby blanket. I didn't even know she could crochet. The skill predates my joining the family. By my best estimates that would make it Precambrian, since

I popped up somewhere in the Mesozoic timeframe. If memory serves, and obviously it doesn't, we're talking Jurassic for me so it's been a good while since she's done any crocheting.

One of the aides asks Gummy to teach her how. I appreciate them so much during moments like this. They know night is her most difficult time of day, so they offer to do something that would involve spending time with her and keeping both her mind and hands busy.

Gummy and I had a good mother-in-law anniversary. We still get along like peas and carrots, or pickles and ice cream.

NOT ONLY DID Gummy paint her church and change her carpet to match my bridesmaids' gowns, but when I *finally* got pregnant, she hosted a huge baby shower for me. The fact that I lived on the other side of the country didn't faze her. Nor did the fact that I couldn't travel, because not only did I suck at getting pregnant, I downright stank at gestating. Most of my pregnancy was spent expanding on the couch under doctor's orders.

Did that stop her? Oh, no it did not. Gummy found a pregnant proxy to stand in for me. Someone videotaped the party. There were games, other people's babies, prizes, and delicious snacks. They looked delicious, anyway. My proxy opened all the gifts and thanked everyone. Gummy rewrapped everything and shipped it all to me in a giant box. Minus potentially delicious snacks.

On top of all that she sent me a check to buy that gorgeous crib I'd lusted after at Macy's so many years previously. The one she tried to bribe me with if I'd hurry up and produce a grandchild. I wasn't above accepting it either, not after years of not-so-subtle hints. Technically I didn't accept the first check, because I lost it. The second check I accepted, after she asked why I'd never cashed the first one and I had to admit to it.

You'd lose your head if it wasn't attached.

Like I never heard that before.

Like I'd let the fact that it's attached stop me from losing my head.

That head may repel paperwork and ignore mail, but it'd never spend that much money on a crib. It insisted on purchasing an entire roomful of unfinished baby furniture and spending months sanding and staining it all.

By sanding and staining it all, I mean supervising Juan at that job.

Can you tell how ridiculously easy-going that mad scientist of mine is? He's super cute too.

When the next baby came and once more it took my complete attention to grow it, Gummy hopped on a plane and came to care for my first-born and visit me in the hospital. When a hot air balloon drifted over the backyard, and the terrified dog hopped through the window to escape the monster, Gummy cleaned up the disaster. She painted the baby's room, hung out with my girlfriends, prepped the house for my return, and gave me the NASA countdown.

My flight home leaves in two weeks.

You'd better have that baby. I have to fly out in one week.

I'm not kidding. Don't you dare not have that baby before I leave on Tuesday.

Can't you jump up and down when the doctors aren't looking?

Fortunately for all involved the baby came just in time. Gummy's time I mean. If I did sneak and jump up and down I'm certainly not going to admit it here.

WE'RE FAST APPROACHING the point of no return.

Now we're getting into the bloody guts of the situation.

We have to sell Gummy's house. For those of you who might someday be in this situation, or heaven forbid already are, let me share a few things you may or may not have learned yet. A year or two of memory care costs most people's entire life savings, including their house. Yes. We absolutely have to sell her house to afford it much longer.

Since Gummy loves rummage sales and thrift stores and hoarding everything, her place is stuffed to the gills with stuff. I want to say junk, but I'm being respectful.

One woman's junk is another woman's treasure.

If I have to dust it, pack it, or touch it, it is junk.

If someone else sells it and puts the money into Gummy's account to pay memory care, then it is treasure.

Months before we moved Gummy to the shire, Juan and I hired a guy to mow her lawn and a woman from the church to clean her house. It amused us how quickly Gummy adapted to a life of luxury. At first she cried when the housekeeper would come, because she wanted to be able to take care of her stuff herself. Maintaining a home is too much for someone who can't remember what chore she is doing, or what day it is.

Thus the housekeeper.

They became fast friends. Soon cleaning day became about fresh baked goods, coffee, and dancing around with lampshades on their heads.

The lawn care service thrilled her. Most of her life she kept her yard in perfectly coiffed shape, with flowers, benches, and her locally famous koi pond. Over the years it had become neglected and overgrown. Once the service began, it again looked neat and almost back to her old standards. Not once did they go about their job without her supervision and cheerleading though.

Those months were dreamy for all of us. Gummy got to stay in her house and a few people were around to help. It wasn't enough.

chapter twenty-two

THE HUMAN RACE

The first time I ever went to the doctor with Gummy happened right after we began suspecting a serious memory problem. I realize now I'd seen the early signs of sundowning on a weekend trip together, but had no idea what it meant. Now I understand we had taken her out of her element, spent long and tiring days driving, and stuck her in a hotel room alone. Nothing was familiar to her. She had no idea what was going on.

Upon returning home, she seemed to get better instantly.

What that meant we weren't sure. Did her memory only get bad in new environments? Would she be safe at home?

Soon after that I made an excuse to travel to her house and go see the doctor with her. Sitting in the waiting room, she filled out the usual forms. Under race she put *Human*, reading it aloud as she did.

Everyone laughed.

No wonder we didn't realize how bad she was for so long. She hid it so well. Looking back I now wonder if she had no idea how to fill out that box.

WE'RE IN THE middle of trying to figure out what is wrong with Gummy's stomach. Her belly is swollen and resembles a woman nearing her third trimester.

Tonight we thought frozen yogurt had the potential superpowers to fix today's problems and pleas to go home.

Gummy digs through her purse as we drive to the frozen yogurt shop. Juan notices her frenetic searching.

> What're you looking for Gummy-Gummy?
>
> My sample.
>
> What sample?
>
> My stool sample. They made me make one, but I don't remember where I put it.

This comes out of the blue. Neither of us knew the stomach investigation had gotten to this point, but it's good that someone somewhere is checking. Since we weren't driving in *my* car with a biological weapon, *I* took it in stride, and found great amusement in Juan's panic. Surely if she'd put a sample in her purse, it would have been obvious to anyone who came near ground zero. However, I certainly won't be the one to go rooting through her purse in the dark car.

Back in the memory care unit, all biosafety measures have been taken. The specimen has been quarantined inside the container it'd been made in. The scientific term is *toilet hat*. In her confusion, but still fastidious, thorough, and neat about such things, Gummy left it on the floor of her room covered in several top-notch and fluffy Target towels.

Disaster averted, and all in all, no one can argue the fact that it was all very ladylike.

IT'S A GOOD thing I have fifteen thousand photos on my phone, because today I have to go through all of them to entertain Gummy. We are in the hospital waiting to have a CT scan done of her abdomen.

Gummy hasn't been allowed to eat or drink, and I pick her hungry, caffeine-free self up too early. I'm not a morning person. She's cooperative as usual when she's getting out. I'm familiar and safe, and more importantly, I'm taking her somewhere.

Fortunately the photo album on my cell isn't just snaps of other people's dogs and travel shots. I also take pictures of pictures. That includes photos of Gummy's photos, and the photos of when my kids were little. So while reminding her to drink whatever nasty they have you ingest before an abdominal CT scan, I entertain her with decades of pictures. Once I run out of pictures, we look up all of her relatives on social media, and then move to Snapchat. Gummy loves these filters, especially the one that makes her look like a deer.

Eventually she stops asking what people do on their phones all the time because she's too busy doing some of it. My storytelling talents do come in handy with Gummy, and I've been part of the family long enough that it isn't much of a stretch. I know a lot of the stories that she's forgotten. I forget things too, but rarely a good story.

After a trip through time with photos, Gummy has mostly stopped repeating herself. Our turn for the CT scan finally comes up. We follow the nurse across the waiting room and Gummy takes over the narrating.

Why he's no taller than me!

Gummy, everyone is taller than you.

He's not! How tall do you think he is? He's not even Asian or anything.

Oh my gosh, look at my sweater. It's covered in lint!

He's just regular. A regular guy and a short one. I've never seen a man that short.

193

I'm dying here. The guy has two perfectly functioning ears. My sweater lint isn't as distracting as *Look! Squirrel!* but it is the best I can come up with on such short and desperate notice.

The nurse has probably heard it all before. He treats Gummy with every kindness. Since she needs a scan, I have to leave the room. They are questioning her when I walk out, and I sneak a picture of her lying there since the ten minute procedure will soon evaporate from her mind. I wait outside and worry that they'll ask her what her symptoms are, and she'll tell them about how healthy she is. The scan will hopefully tell the truth for her. She's unlikely to be asked for her social security number at this point. It was an issue at another appointment this week.

It has a seven in it. Um. Seven. Seven. Four. Seven. Four. Four. Seven. Four. Seven. Seven. Four. Seven. Four. Seven. Seven. Does that sound right?

Gummy expends a lot of her energy trying to pass in the outside world. It seems like it's worth it if she gets a positive experience from the effort, like watching a sporting event, easy movie, or spending time with a group of people who lift her spirits. The hospital doesn't fit into that category. No sooner do we get into the car than she asks me to look at her spit, and sticks out her tongue to show off stringy spittle. She somehow manages to talk with her tongue still hanging out.

What's wrong with my spit?

You haven't had anything to drink today. We're going to go get you something now, and some lunch.

This is where I'm the worst at caregiving. I forgot to bring a bottle of water. I leave her purse behind regularly. Don't bring a warm coat. Don't notice she's wearing slippers. Things like that. Though, thanks to my phone and tens of thousands of pictures, I've got the dog and pony show down!

We go to a fried chicken place for lunch. Gummy adores fried stuff. She drinks a huge soda and eats her chicken, and completely forgets where she's been or why. I notice she is breaking out in hives, something she's dealt with for years, although she doesn't seem to remember it today. Rather than take her back to assisted living, I take her over to my house, hoping she can relax and drink enough to fix her spit problem.

Do people with severe memory loss ever truly relax? Gummy doesn't. She ramps up the pacing, sharking around my house on a quest for something to do. By now her belly is sticking out like she is entering her third trimester. The gurgling and growling coming from it could be used in a horror movie. They never get that right in the movies, do they? They never realize that the alien inside would be heard from the outside. Gummy could tell them.

Rather than spending the entire afternoon with her asking *what do you want me to do now? Could you give me a ride home?* I decide to make pumpkin rolls. Thanksgiving is coming. Pumpkin rolls were always Gummy's thing. She loves them, and used to make a bunch and freeze them. I've been buying her slices at the supermarket and taking them to her in the evenings. Homemade would be way better.

This is how colossally stupid my brain is sometimes. Poor choices are not only in the realm of the brain impaired.

BAKING ISN'T MY thing. With Gummy sharking around and asking questions, it feels like purgatory. As soon as I take the pumpkin roll pans out of the oven and get them on kitchen towels to cool, I usher Gummy out the door. All the way back to memory care I answer her questions with whatever will make her move fastest.

What's this place?

You'll see in a minute. Hey, look at that beautiful wreath!

That's nice. Where are you taking me?

I'll take you wherever you want to go, Gummy, but we need to stop at this place right now.

Telling Gummy what she needs to hear bothers me less as time goes on. My tolerance level for lying goes up depending on how tired I am and how uncooperative or confused Gummy is. It seems to me that people worried too much about deceiving people with dementia or Alzheimer's haven't had any real exposure to it.

You could spend the rest of your natural life trying to explain what is really going on, only to be met with the necessity of repeating it forever. Even after you explain, your words will be rejected for the reality they perceive.

Will you tell them each and every time they forget that loved ones died? That they're old? That their mind isn't functioning like it used to? All of their time would be spent in hysterical tears or furious rebuffs.

Did you see *Fifty First Dates*? Gummy often slips into Ten Second Tom mode. There isn't enough time to explain reality before the brain misfires and the questions begin again. Trying to cram reality into the brain of someone with dementia or Alzheimer's seems to be more for the satisfaction of those not suffering it.

THE NEXT TIME I go to visit Gummy, she is already sundowning. Keeping her busy putting together a puzzle helps a little. She reminds me she is ready to go home, and is adamant she isn't coming back here anytime soon. After a couple grandkids, Facetime, and visitors, she relaxes slightly and begins to go with the flow.

That's something she does often. I think her generation is much more cooperative, civic-minded, and prone to waiting their turn than newer generations. At an assisted living picnic I didn't hear a single complaint, despite four hundred people making their way through the slow lines to get lunch.

When I ask Gummy if she wants a hamburger or a hotdog or an apple or an orange, she is willing to go with whatever I pick. She insists she isn't picky. And she's not. Her only preference is Pepsi. But she'll accept ginger ale without complaint, and only dis on Coke a wee bit.

I shudder to picture generations with less patience going through this. Let's hope for a cure, and not just because grande caramel macchiato decaf with sprinkles won't be on the menu, but because even spoiled and picky people deserve to keep their minds intact.

Unfortunately we don't get what we deserve. We get what we get.

chapter twenty-three

BORN ON THE FOURTH OF JULY

The good thing about being born on the Fourth of July is always getting your birthday off. Gummy has always had a party, even if she got stuck with all the planning. No matter what, she was always in charge. I learned that quickly the first time.

Poppy, you take the cooler. Juan, you carry the towels.

Did you all bring your swimsuits?

We did, Gummy.

Good. Saffi, you take the—look at you! Did you do your hair?

Yes.

You did your hair to go swimming? Why?

It was bugging me. I'll keep it out of the pool.

Good luck with that. Juan drags everyone under. If you stick around long enough, you'll learn not to get dolled up for family picnics.

He'd better not pull me under.

He pulls everyone under. Being his girlfriend won't save you.

He won't pull me under.

Well, maybe not. You can pull the no-sex card on him.

Insert awk-weird silence here. My boyfriend's mother announced this in front of his entire family. I can't believe she said it, even if it is true.

An hour later we unload coolers and leave them on picnic tables at the park. Gummy and Poppy spent the last half hour of the drive arguing over who forgot the meatloaf at the house. The guys drag him off before it gets any more heated, and Gummy digs through the coolers one more time hoping to find it. Giving up, she grabs her beach bag.

Let's go swimming.

Are we just leaving everything here?

Yeah. It'll be fine.

No one will steal it?

No! Why would they do that? Get your towel. Let's go.

I pick up my towel and bag.

I can't believe no one will bother anything.

They never have in all the years we've been coming here. I still can't believe you fixed your hair to go swimming.

I can't believe Poppy forgot the meatloaf.

That man drives me crazy. He had me up making that at midnight. Now we'll have to throw it away after it sits out all day.

I can't believe you were up making meatloaf in the middle of the night!

Making meatloaf in the middle of the night? Is that what they call it now? That's not what they called it when I used to do it.

She laughs when I don't know how to respond.

THE FOURTH OF July weekend drags by, long and hot. This year, instead of fireworks and picnics, I'm sitting in the bushes on a mountain picking blueberries with the birthday girl. She's carrying a bucket almost full of Juan's favorite berries. I'm literally sitting on the ground, figuratively melting, and painstakingly picking all the bushes within arm's reach. Gummy is moving around, squatting down to a crouch and moving from bush to bush, picking as fast as a machine without ever fully standing. She gets leaves and bits of twigs too, but says when she soaks the berries these bits will rise to the top and be easy to remove.

We don't have all day.

I know. We have all weekend.

Don't be a smart ass. I have to clean that cabin, and I'm going to make a pie.

The only thing worse than being in a tar paper box on top of a mountain on the hottest day of the year, is baking in it too. I'm not hurrying. I'm sitting in the shade. I don't mind half-heartedly picking berries with Gummy, but I have no interest in baking.

Once the bushes closest to me have been picked through, I run my hands over them one last time, hoping to find a reason not to move. Noticing milkweed growing beside them, I shoot to my feet.

Oh, my God, there is larva on this!

What's wrong?

Gummy jogs over to look.

Just smash that.

Are you kidding? This is a Monarch Butterfly caterpillar! The whole plant is covered in them! Look at that! There's a chrysalis on that leaf! You can see the butterfly inside.

They're butterfly bugs?

Yeah, the kids and I used to raise them in Texas. I always found them there in April, but I guess they're here in July! Look, there's another plant here. I need an empty bucket.

Mine are full of berries.

I dump my blueberries into her bucket and start picking the sticky leaves off the plant. They're covered in the black, white, and yellow striped caterpillars. I fill the bucket with them and milkweed.

What on earth are you going to do with those?

I'm going to feed them, raise them, and when they turn into butterflies, I'm going to tag them for the Monarch Watch program.

You're what?

You get these tiny little stickers you put on one wing and you let them go, but it helps track them. I can't believe I found them. There's a butterfly!

That big orange one?

Yes. That's a Monarch.

I see that kind here all of the time.

That one's a boy.

How do you know?

The bottom two wings of the males have dots on them.

201

Those are his boy bits? Wow. Wait here. I've got bags in
the car that we can put the berries in. I want to see these
things turn into butterflies.

Starting that weekend and then for many years after, we spent summers foraging for butterfly eggs or caterpillars rather than berries.

Gummy loved to give me crap, but I will admit she always got on board with any idea I came up with. She even made all the guys help.

GUMMY IS A clever, fierce, sweetheart of a woman, a lovely human being, and like so many others, struggling through each day with this cruel disease. Born on the Fourth of July, her dollop of Little Miss Sassy Pants comes in handy when she's staging a coup in the memory care facility.

Today Gummy has a date with one of my kids. There's a nearby ceramics studio that allows customers to select an item and paint it on the premises. Gummy has gone a couple times now, and each time she wanders the aisles looking at unpainted pieces, worrying out loud—and I imagine in her head too—about how she can't remember how to paint anymore and wondering which one she should pick.

Today she picks two pieces that I'd call complicated. They're mice angels. Before, I'd have encouraged her to pick something simpler. Sometimes we choose for her because a decision is too overwhelming. This time I let her choose. A momentous thing in and of itself. Picking paint becomes complex. I worry the woman pouring paint will lose her patience. There's no good way for me to point out Gummy has dementia and to give her a break.

Eventually we all settle at a table to paint. For over an hour Gummy paints those pieces, starting with a dark grey, then dry brushing a lighter coat, and working on the eyes with meticulous patience. This is a good day. Gummy did something normal. She knew how to do it. In fact, she's still quite good. We have to leave the pieces there unfinished, which she has a problem with.

I could finish those at home.

We can finish them the day after tomorrow.

I'd rather take them home and do them there.

That's all the arguing she does though. She grabs her coat and puts it on, finds her purse and hoists it over her shoulder.

Look at that statue of Elvis! I'd like to paint that one.

You should get it next time.

That's too expensive.

She's in a good mood as we say goodbye to the grandkids and leave. She stops at Cinnabon before we walk out the door, checking out the free samples, and talks to the guy behind the counter.

Do you mind if I take one? They smell great.

Help yourself! That's what they're there for.

Thank you.

Would you like to get one to take home?

No, thank you. I don't want to ruin my girlish figure.

She pats her hips and the young guy stares at her, a bit slack-jawed, as she sashays toward the mall exit. I follow her.

You know what I need to do? I need to get up in my attic and drag down my Christmas decorations and I need to put them up. I haven't been doing anything lately. I need to do things.

All the way back to assisted living Gummy chats about her sons and family. Typically she is confused when we arrive at assisted living, and we have to come up with a reason to get her inside and to her unit, but she follows me willingly, talking. We walk into her unit and an aide greets her.

Hi, Gummy. What have you been up to?

I was painting ceramics.

She calls the aide by name. That's not that unusual; she thinks she knows them all from church, or the mall, or Burger King. But today she calls her by the *correct* name! *What?* She remembered! I don't know how it will go when we do this next time. I don't know if she'll remember it or not, but for tonight this is a big win.

GUMMY RECOGNIZES EVERY single article of her clothing. It's one of the most ironic things when she can't recognize where she's living, but knows every sock and shoe. When the laundry doesn't return something, she goes on a little rampage.

They keep my stuff.

Your name has to be inside everything that goes into the hamper. That's how they know who to give it to.

Nobody told me.

She takes her dirty clothes out of the hamper and jams them into her closet.

I'll wash everything when I get home.

Let me write your name on them. I have a Sharpie in my purse.

You don't have to. I'm going home tomorrow.

But it's one less thing for you to wash when you get there. They're really fast. If we put it in the laundry tonight, you'll have it back in the morning.

Oh, that's what they say, but I have *three things* missing.

She never wants to wear new stuff because she thinks it isn't hers. I bought her a beautiful outfit she keeps in her closet and pulls out to admire from time to time. I tell her it's hers and she gushes over it, but never wears it. She can't remember it belongs to her long enough.

Gummy has a notebook with everyone's phone numbers in it. It vanishes with her purse from time to time, but she tries to keep it with her.

This past week I've added a large weekly calendar and filled it with what we're doing each day. Some days it says *Day Club* to remind her which days she goes there, or *Church*. I ask my kids to help me fill it in with something, so she always has something to look forward to. Other days it has *Ceramics* or *Football* on it. Some days it just says who will call her that day. She's now keeping it with her purse, phone book, and important papers.

Today we go out to dinner again. I have *got* to stop eating out two times a week with her. At least I choose a veggie dish. Gummy first considers a salad, and then caves when she spots the burgers. Of course she took half of her burger to go, but the small victory of the day is she did not put it in her purse. Although my kids brought her to dinner, I offer to drive her back. I'm pretty thrilled when they take time to do things with her, but she has to be walked back to her room, acclimated to it, convinced to stay, and preoccupied enough to not follow you back out—and that takes a lot of time. More time than they usually have.

Writers have that time. Hypothetically.

Not true at all. I have that time because I'm not writing.

Gummy's been in assisted living for months now, and she is getting more comfortable with it. Most evenings she sits and chats and works on puzzles with other residents. Knowing that does my heart good. It gives me hope that given enough time, she will adjust.

Tonight she doesn't recognize the assisted living facility, or the memory care unit.

Where are we going?

It's right up the next hall.

I need to get home.

I know.

205

Where are you taking me?

Just up the next hall.

I'm gonna need a ride home after this.

Okay.

What is this place?

It's assisted living.

I don't know what that is.

It's for senior citizens.

Nobody told me.

After all that arguing, she points at her door.

That's my room. All I do is sit in that room.

Baby steps.

She pats my arm as the old Gummy makes an appearance and steps through the dementia again.

Saffi. You're very good to me.

You've always been very good to me too, Gummy.

I love you. You know that.

I know. I love you too. You've been the best mother-in-law.
You know sometimes you're the only reason I put up with
Juan's crap.

I couldn't love you more if you'd been born my own
daughter.

I love you too, Gummy.

It takes me a minute to get away and out the door of the memory care unit. Someone has to plug the code in. I know the code, but they don't know that. I watch them when they plug it in and memorize it. I don't dare punch it in with Little-Miss-Still-Remembers-Phone-Numbers Gummy watching. I'm sure if anything is going to stick in her memory, this code is it. I have to wait for someone to come over and ask how our outing went. I suppose they're used to watching family cry, the same way they're used to having to guard that code with their life from the inhabitants of the memory care unit. There's almost always a resident sharking back and forth in front of the door hoping to escape. Face it, it's normal. If people with dementia do nothing else normal, the desire to get back home to the familiar is one thing they do that is absolutely and perfectly normal.

As soon as I make it to the stairs I start to sob. This sucks, because today has been a perfect day.

I cry all the way home. I know Gummy knows, in some deep intrinsic part of her, that she's slipping away day by day. But at least we have these moments before she goes. I've noticed when someone has a life threatening event, they're the ones who will say *I love you* or tell you the truth about how they feel. They know life is short.

She's not the only one who knows.

THE MEMORIES ARE everywhere.

Gummy and I cozy up on the couch for hours with my sleeping baby. We've definitely bonded over this ability to never get bored with watching and interpreting the faintest of facial expressions.

Did you see that? That means they're dreaming!

You can tell it's a happy dream!

It's so sweet! You should have another one really fast!

Juan groans as he walks past us.

Mom!

We reply in unison.

What?!

The clock chimes eight. My firstborn, all sweet in fuzzy yellow footed jammies, toddles around the living room playing with Gummy. I interrupt.

Clock says bedtime!

Gummy shoots me a dirty look, but my toddler obediently heads for his room and crib. He stands beside it, waiting to be lifted in.

Oh, come on! You don't know what it's like to have a baby yet. Just you wait for the next one.

I don't say what I'm thinking. It really isn't that hard. I pull the bedroom door almost shut and whisper to her.

I read the baby book. It said to blame bedtime on the clock. That's why I say 'clock says' for bath time and bedtime.

Unless your kid is reading the book too, I don't care what it says. Wait for the next kid. That isn't a real baby.

Turns out Gummy was right, but I didn't know it for another year.

I'm a little doll who was dropped and broken...

As I rock in the rocking chair, a tiny hand comes up to cover my mouth and stop my singing.

No, Mommy. Gummy sing. I want Gummy sing.

Fine! Gummy definitely gets top billing in the singing department. Even my big boy still wants Gummy to come sing and do the nightly tuck into bed. I'm glad to have the evening off, but dang it on the song front.

It's midnight at Gummy's house. My son is marching around wearing Mickey Mouse underwear and pounding on a drum. My daughter is sitting in her diaper at the organ, smacking the keys. Everyone is singing. Loudly. The windows are open and I'm surprised the neighbors don't have something to say about this.

It's midnight at our first house in Texas. The baby is sick and screaming. The toddler is sick and puking. Juan had surgery and is stumping around wearing a hip to toe cast, carrying the bathroom garbage can. He caught the bug too. My head is pounding and my stomach feels queasy. Gummy just flew halfway across the country and is taking care of both kids and her son, and *smiling*.

Go to bed, Saffi.

I can't leave you with this mess.

Oh, I've had messes before. I'm fine. Go to bed.

God, I love that woman.

It seems like there are decades of memories of little moments. Gummy and I selecting paint or supplies for our latest project. Hot air balloon festivals. Art shows and craft fairs. Museums. Libraries. Zoos. Almost always with kids in tow. Juan and I arriving at their house after midnight only to find Gummy painting and Poppy prepping tomorrow's dinner or canning tomatoes. It seemed strange at first, and then it didn't, and given enough time Juan and I have begun to follow their example. Maybe he's putting line on fishing poles and I'm writing at one in the morning, but apparently the refusal to allow time to constrain you is contagious.

Sometime during the past eighty million years we've been tossed together, I went from trying to avoid Gummy and being annoyed with her to begrudging admiration and eventually outright affection. How can I not respect this woman who brought such a good, kind—and let's be real, occasionally annoying—man into my life.

If your spouse hunts and fishes, I know you understand.

Fact is I adore them both. Except when I don't.

chapter twenty-four

THE UGLY BITS

I t's the Thanksgiving prep that I can't seem to get out from under. We're prepping for a Griswold Rockwellian Thanksgiving right here at my house. Holidays mean Gummy and Poppy time even with more than half of them gone.

This year it's just Gummy with us, and for the first time she's not traveling to get here. She lives here. Although she's having trouble with that concept, we're hoping the gathering will be familiar at least. It's the first holiday we have celebrated since Gummy moved to the shire.

Gummy, do you want anything special for Thanksgiving?

A man.

Does this mean I get to pick one for you?

No. I have enough problems. Make whatever you want. I'll help.

If I'm doing it my way, we'd have ice cream and salad for Thanksgiving dinner.

I'm not picky, make what you want. You're going to make good corn though, right? That's my favorite part.

What kind of corn is good corn exactly?

I had to ask that because corn wasn't on the traditional menu.

Well, now. It's best if you grow it yourself.

It's kind of late for that. Thanksgiving is the day after tomorrow.

She laughs.

You need to plan ahead! I grow it myself, cut it off the cob and parboil it, then freeze it. If you can't do that, just open a can of corn. I'm not picky.

Yeah, right, not picky. Grow it yourself?! Still, I ran to Target after dropping Gummy back at assisted living, and I bought the damn corn. Frozen. Very upscale.

I am planning Thanksgiving dinner because I love my family. I'm not one of those women who relish this. I love the family time, but I don't like the cooking and baking stuff. I think it would be perfectly acceptable to go to one of those posh hotels or a winery for a nice Thanksgiving buffet. Every year that idea gets soundly nixed. They want leftovers. Everyone wants to eat leftovers into the weekend, until they can't bear it another day. It's tradition.

This holiday is tucked between finishing up a novel that's due in the next few days and Juan about to embark on another trip to Asia, with a double stuffed filling of dementia in the middle. In keeping with the spirit of the holiday, assisted living has an early Thanksgiving for families and residents. A locally famous chef produces three meals a day for the residents, so you never hear anyone fussing about the food. It explains how Gummy has gained fourteen pounds since she got here.

That's a good thing. I'm fairly certain she sometimes went from forgetting to eat, to those less-than-a-dollar cellophane-wrapped garbage snacks for three meals a day.

Juan and I arrive at the assisted living special family Thanksgiving event. Seating is limited so the entire family can't attend. We sit at a dining table in the room where Gummy goes to Sittercise and church.

> Now this place looks familiar.
>
> *It's where you go to church.*
>
> That's right. But only on Sundays. I come here for other classes too, and this is where we went to the craft show the other day. I took down that Christmas wreath you bought for my door. I'm hoping I can go home by Christmas. I've been here, what—almost three months now, right?

Neither Juan nor I answer for several beats. Our jaws are almost literally in our laps.

We stay for hours. Gummy is asking smart questions and wants a tour of the facility. Juan, my practical mad scientist, points out we'd done it before.

> We've given you this tour before, Gummy.
>
> Yes, I remember, but this is the first time I understood where I was. I thought I was in my town before. Now I need to get my bearings.

We proceed to walk the facility. So many families came for the dinner that the elevators are backed up, so we take the stairs.

> You know your way around here, Saffi, because you're a snoop. I wouldn't go through these doors on my own, but you'll march in anywhere won't you?
>
> *Pretty much. I got it from my mother-in-law.*

I'll slap your ass. Explain this to me. Some of the people who live here have health problems, and some are in memory care like me, and some are fine?

Pause for another jaw drop here.

By the time we return to Gummy's room, the post-turkey tryptophan is kicking in, combined with feeling rather like Alice through the rabbit hole, where nothing is as it seems. *This* with-it woman is my mother-in-law. I don't know where she's been, but she's going to kick my ass for putting her into a memory care unit.

Juan starts rooting through her drawers for the remote. Gummy opens a bedside table and hands it to him. My jaw is still slack. This is a perfectly normal, very un-dementia-affected place to put her remote. Juan and I look around the room. There are no stacks of clothing, no packed bags, and no evident escape routes mapped out.

> Don't I have some things I made at the ceramics place at the mall? Aren't they getting glazed? They should be done by now.
>
> *They are, Gummy. You're right!*
>
> I have two angel mice I didn't finish painting. When are we going to go do that?
>
> *I was thinking next week, after Thanksgiving. Can you wait that long?*
>
> Yeah, I can probably wait.

We talk about our upcoming holiday plans. We used to go blow glass at Thanksgiving, but last year Gummy reached for the molten hot glass. She has to touch everything. I'm not even sure how much of that is dementia, because she's always been like that. This year all fiery lava-like substances are out.

Once more I take her notebook and write all the days of the week down and what she'll be doing each of those days. She's continued to refer to this calendar over the past couple weeks. Even the times she picks up an old list, or goes on the wrong page, it still seems to help her get her bearings. Today she hardly seems to need it.

THESE MOMENTS OF clarity are gifts. They don't last. Gummy calls me the next day asking for a ride home from the store.

On the agenda today is painting ceramics with one of my kids. I pick Gummy up. She is wearing the jeans and striped sweater that she wears at least every other day, if not more often. It's bitter cold outside, and as I circle the parking lot it occurs to me that this will be a problem when taking her out in the winter. I wonder if there's a way to get a handicap permit to use when she's with me.

It isn't likely I'll pursue that. I'd rather wrap her in a blanket and carry her through the parking lot at a run than fool with the DMV for anything. With as much as I travel and trot through strange cities late at night, I usually have a mugging scenario in my head. A robber can have all my stuff, but a certain amount of begging might commence when it comes to giving up my license. Please, please, please don't make me go to the DMV. I've had to start carrying Gummy's driver's license too. When she checks in for medical procedures at the hospital, they always want photo identification. Now I have double the fear of having to spend the rest of Gummy's remaining good years in line at the DMV.

We walk into the mall at the perfect time. Free samples at Cinnabon once more. Gummy's memory isn't great today, but it's not her worst. She sits down at the ceramic studio and drifts away to dry brushing her angel mice to perfection. I remind her about the time she brought ceramics to my big house in Texas. Yes, our previous homes are defined as the little house that got ruined by the tornado, and the big house where Gummy let the kids paint ceramics on my kitchen table. I'm still not certain which house suffered more damage.

I remember the kids painted everything black or blue.

I remember that too!

I still remember my little one crying. She kept saying the eyes she tried to paint were wrong and her hands wouldn't listen.

I know that feeling. My hands won't listen today.

Your mice look great.

I used to be able to paint even better.

Years ago Gummy and her best friend lamented their loss of beauty to me. I remember it as one of the singularly most hysterical conversations I've taken part in.

You don't know what it's like to get older for a woman.

People treat you differently.

Yeah, you become invisible.

Or worse.

You both have more to offer the world than your looks.

Don't change the subject, Saffi.

No one asks for your resume. They look at you and judge.

They do that no matter how old you are!

You don't understand. She doesn't understand.

Well, she never had really great looks like we did, so she can't.

Now that's true. We were both great beauties.

I think about bringing up that conversation, but it's getting late and sundowning is beginning, so I let it go. Irony rarely translates into sundowning. My storytelling memories for Gummy need to be short and simple ones, especially late at night.

I keep the memory to myself and chuckle for a bit. Looks seem so important, but they fade. Life skills seem so important, but they falter and fade too. Memory seems so important, but for many that fades too in the end. What's left? A person. Someone with needs and hopes.

Gummy sits across from me at Friendly's again. It is fishamajig sandwich time again, and yes, she is wrapping the second half of her sandwich and tucking it into her purse.

They're really not coming?

No, Gummy. I'm sorry.

Why not?

I don't know why. Do you want more ketchup?

It's the best I can do. I'm attempting distraction like one does for a toddler who wants a candy bar in the checkout aisle. Gummy wants company. I'm not sure where she is in time, but someone isn't here who she thinks should be. I'm rolling with it. There are big tears in her eyes, but she blinks them back.

I guess they don't really like me.

Everybody likes you, Gummy. Even your daughter-in-law.

Does she?

Sigh. This isn't paint by numbers. This isn't right or wrong. It's confusion all the way to the horizon, with lots of stabbing in the dark. And even in the midst of all this chaos I know I lucked into one of the best mothers-in-law ever.

The sun is setting as we hurry across the parking lot in bitter wind. I hit the button to start my Jeep and put one arm around Gummy's shoulders. Usually I have excellent parking karma, and can almost always score an upfront parking spot. It drives my kids nuts. Truthfully, since I write for a living, most of which is done late at night, I can run errands during off hours. Sometimes I run them late at night just before closing. It's easy to park at the mall fifteen minutes before closing.

I think I lost my water.

Immediately I know what she's being so ladylike about.

It's okay, Gummy. It happens.

Gummy looks at me, stricken. Mentally I kick myself. This is the type of situation where I really stink at being caregiver. Why didn't I take her to the bathroom? We'd been there for hours! I didn't think to push her when she said she didn't have to go.

This is a tough relationship. I'm the daughter-in-law. It's hard to tell Gummy when to use the restroom. I'm too used to the way she's been all these years before. Sometimes I thought she was the only female in the world who could manage to pee only two or three times a day.

In terms of water output Gummy is a human camel. I'm an anxious terrier. She'd always had to endure my mad dashes through a mall or when I'd arrive for a visit and bellow a hello as I raced to the bathroom. I can remember her standing outside my stall at a public restroom giving me grief.

You need to see a doctor.

I'm fine, Gummy.

Is it your time of the month?

Are you keeping track?

Don't be a smart mouth. Nobody has to pee this much.

I think iced tea with lemon bypasses my kidneys.

Maybe you shouldn't drink it

This has never happened before. Incontinence often goes hand in hand with memory problems. They just forget. Of all the facts and bits I've written in here, this is the hardest for me to be candid about. Sometimes you *have* to pee, and when I have to, I'd like to burn down every gas station that denies restroom usage to frantic travelers. The humiliation is familiar.

At assisted living I park right by the front doors and usher her in. The accident has upset her thinking.

> Where is this place?
>
> Are you going to leave me here?
>
> Just help me remember. Why am I in this place?

I explain as we make our way to her floor and the memory care unit.

> I don't remember any of this, Saffi.
>
> *You will, Gummy. I promise. And I'm not going to leave you until you're okay.*

We enter the memory care unit and she spots a familiar face and relaxes a bit. She's still not certain why she's here or where she is, but she knows this place. In her room she begins formulating theories of why she has this room. We're not at Burger King now. We're in a room her husband rented in some city years ago. It's not based in a reality I know, but that doesn't mean it isn't based in one.

> I've never wet myself before.
>
> *You're one of the lucky ones, Gummy. I did it about a month ago.*
>
> Did you really?
>
> *I swear to God I did. I don't know how. I drove thirty miles holding it, then arrived home, put my hand on the bathroom doorknob, and my bladder got so thrilled it couldn't wait.*

Gummy chuckles, but her eyes are worried.

> *I'm sorry I didn't take you to the bathroom. This isn't your fault. It really is okay.*
>
> Are you going to leave? Can you sleep here with me?

These are the comments that rip your guts out. The mother in me wants to bring Gummy back to my house, tuck her into the spare room bed, and keep her there. But we've done that. I know how that story goes. It winds up right here. It's hard to leave knowing that she's scared here, but it doesn't usually take much to make her more comfortable.

I took off my coat.

I can't stay here all night, Gummy.

Okay.

But let's find some warm pajamas, and I'll run you a hot bath. You'll see me or Juan tomorrow, and after that is Thanksgiving. You'll spend that whole day at my house.

I'm going to your house?

Yes, you are.

Within fifteen minutes we've sorted through her drawers. The bath is run. Gummy sharks in circles for a little longer. I slowly herd her into the bathroom while the water is still hot. She hands me her dirty clothes.

Now what are you going to do with those?

I'm going to send them to the laundry. There's a service here. You'll get them back tomorrow.

Huh, so they say. I sent three things down and they've never come back.

I know this story. She still hasn't forgotten the things that have gone missing.

These will come back because I'm going to make sure your name is written in them.

Well, okay. But you don't have to stay here while I take a bath.

Okay, I'll see you later. I love you.

I love you too, Saffi. Good night.

As I head out the door, she shouts that she loves me a couple more times. I grab a fabric pen from the staff's station, write her name inside her dirty clothes, and put them into the laundry. I stop at Target to buy warm pajamas for her—likely a futile mission since she is afraid to wear things she doesn't recognize—and am driving home when I remember the effing fish sandwich in her purse. I call and ask for a specific aide.

Hey, hi! It's Saffi. Gummy and I went out for fishamajig sandwiches again today. Do I even have to say it?

I'll get it out of her purse. You have a good evening.

You too. Thanks!

chapter twenty-five

THANKFUL

The staff has recently given Gummy the nickname of Patty Mayonnaise. She kind of likes it. I had to look it up. She's a cartoon side character, a girl crush everyone likes. The staff treats memory care residents like any other person, but with a good deal more patience. As we are walking out of the building today, we run into a staff member. Gummy launches into complaints about how she's stuck sitting around there all day long, and this outing with me is the first thing she's done in weeks.

The staff member sighs.

> Please. You're like my Maltese. Whenever somebody comes over he leans against them, *Nobody feeds me! I'm hungry! I'm lonely! They never pet me!*

That cracks me and Gummy up. She can be like that. They all can. In fact, we all do it. I suppose it is the human equivalent of, *Pet me again!*

Early on in our relationship, during one of those innumerous times we were thrown together, Gummy got annoyed with me. The particulars have gotten lost in time. It's the words that stayed with me.

Saffi. Saffi. Saffi. I'm so sick of hearing that! Why's every-thing always about Saffi? What about Gummy?

I recall my surprise at such a childish reaction, and turning my atten-tion to the guys to see how they would handle it. They took off. They weren't touching that one. So the way I handled it was typical for me at that time. I discussed it with my girlfriends. There's nothing like getting with the girl-friend coven for circumventing progress with the mother-in-law. Now, with Gummy at her worst, I'm much more apt to face anger directly, searching for the source. Not that that would have been relevant at the time, because knowing Gummy as I do now, I realize she was joking. I was the childish one, quick to judge before really getting to know her.

Gummy is having a nice Thanksgiving, despite it being a ghost of the usual over-the-top holiday celebrations we've had. We have traditions. I freak out over the details for a couple weeks ahead of time. My house gets the *Company is Coming* cleaning that helps keep it above health code violations. I stock up on silly things like chocolate turkeys, and sparkles and glitter glue to make seating cards. We eat a huge dinner that usually turns out fairly well, and there are enough leftovers for everyone to take some home because I go way overboard. Always.

Juan and Gummy clean up afterward. I've never let Gummy help cook anything, because I stink at multi-tasking and I've always prepped everything well in advance. She has a strict sense of fairness. If I cooked it all, she has to clean it all. This has worked beautifully for me over the years. Peas and carrots.

On Gummy's calendar for this week I've written, *Thanksgiving at Saf-fi's house! Dress cute!* With a little help from the staff in memory care this happens. Gummy arrives wearing a floaty purple top and matching pants *and heels!* Her hair has just been styled, as it is every week by a stylist at the facility, although Gummy never remembers and complains about it often.

Gummy, you look so nice!

Oh! This? I've had this! What do you want me to do?

Get yourself something to drink and help us eat all of this food.

Well, you know I can't eat a lot at once, but if you give me a few hours I could probably do it.

Don't believe her. She couldn't do it, but she eats and chats away. After dinner we decide the best way to burn those extra calories is to sit in front of the television and watch a movie. One of my kids chooses *Finding Dory*. It seems like a family friendly movie, and a colorful one that Gummy will probably enjoy.

Finding Dory turns out to be perfect for someone with memory problems. A forgetful little fish trying to find her way home—metaphor much? What has Gummy been doing the last few months other than trying to get home? Throughout the entire movie Dory has trouble because she can't remember things. During the movie we all exchange meaningful looks. *Could this be more perfect? Is it going to bother her?* We watch as Gummy scoots to the edge of the sofa, wrapped in an electric throw to keep her warm, and hangs onto every word of the movie.

I love that Dory's friends helped her when she got lost, and no one judges her memory problem. Dory herself is the hero though, because she never gives up. She tries and tries.

At the end of the movie, Gummy at last relaxes back against the sofa and looks around.

We're all grown-ups. I can't believe we sat here and watched that kid movie!

Throughout our Thanksgiving celebration, Gummy stays a bit more grounded than usual, or at least fakes it well as she is apt to do in a familiar social setting. As the day progresses she isn't certain why we are there—or where we are. Once early darkness falls, she begins to chase her tail, searching for the edges of her memory to hold onto.

Now who all is here?

Just us, Gummy.

No kids?

Nope, no kids.

Okay. And when am I going home?

In a little bit. Are you in a hurry to go?

No. No, I'm not in a hurry. I'm just trying to figure out where I should be. Where am I going when I leave?

Home to your apartment.

What apartment?

And round and round we go, explaining.

The biggest victory of the day comes when we take Gummy back to assisted living, and she recognizes the building from the outside as someplace she knows. This is a first.

Entering the memory care unit, Gummy lights up, happy to be in more familiar territory. For once, she is more comfortable back in memory care than at my house.

This victory tells me two things. Gummy can still adapt and retain new information—given the right set of circumstances and a whole heck of a lot of patience. And that I should probably bring her over my house a bit more often. Family is a comforting balm for confusion. At least while we're still familiar.

Lately I've had people comment that I'm very patient with Gummy, or very kind to her. The truth is I can be a wildly impatient person. Being a care-giver does not come easily. I've been using up all my patience on Gummy, and I really don't have much left over.

Ask Juan. He's the patient one. If I rant about the injustice of paperwork, he steps in and helps me. If I bring him a Panera salad for the fourth time this week because I haven't taken the time to cook, he thanks me. If I read, see, or hear something that upsets me, he can always talk it into the logic column for me. He's the Saffi Whisperer. Juan and time have taught me that it's never in my best interest to follow through on impatient impulses.

My only skill for this job is I'm empathetic.

There have been times when we're sitting in the doctor's office, Gummy with her swelled up gassy belly will be burping to make her sons proud, and I'll start to burp. It's ridiculous. Other times she will be grasping for words and I know what she's trying to say.

The odd thing is I get more out of this relationship than I put in. You wouldn't think it at first, and it isn't always the case. There are big chunks of time when she about kills me and I have to stay away to recharge. But I'm drawn back to her every time. It's that love thing. It's that deep respect thing. On some cosmic level it is my responsibility.

There is a deep visceral satisfaction in helping someone, especially if service is your love language. I do believe in karma. Not as in, if I'm helpful to Gummy then someone will be helpful to me in the same circumstances that would literally strike me as bad karma, trying to stack the odds for self-serving purposes. It's more that if I'm helpful to Gummy, I've put that much honor and good into this messy and chaotic world. My effort ideally goes into the positive column, and we need more of that. The more of that in the world, the better for all of us.

There are also selfish reasons. If I can get Gummy happy and settled, taking care of her will be easier. My family will be happier.

There is also the most selfish reason of all. It didn't occur to me at first. Writing and sharing about Gummy is physically painful, but writing is cathartic for me, and our story has been beating on my heart for a long time. My dream is to make lemonade from these lemons, but my heart says, "Hey, Saffi, what will you do with all the blood and tears?"

I AM HAPPY to report that Gummy has had a whole lot more good than bad lately. I don't know if the memory medicine is at last slowing the progression of dementia, or if painting ceramics a couple times a week is that therapeutic, but she is happier.

After painting ceramics, Gummy is usually beginning to sundown, but she's calmer and hangs onto threads of real world. She might not know where she is, or why, or even when, but she'll grab onto something real and focus on it—like the beauty of the drive we're taking, or something she really did that week, or talking about someone she loves in a realistic way.

It feels very much like hanging onto some shard of reality while drifting through a storm, but it centers her.

The written schedule seems to help too. Gummy refers to it throughout the week and always has someone familiar to get excited about seeing, or an activity to attend, and therefore a lot of things to look forward to each week.

When her calendar is coupled with the activities at assisted living, she has a full schedule.

One night last week I called Gummy and she answered, out of breath. Her room is across the hall from the lounge and she'd run to get the phone. "I can't talk long. I'm building a puzzle with my friends." It was the best moment of my life in a long time. I couldn't wait for Juan to get home so I could tell him Gummy couldn't chat tonight because she was busy with her friends.

I'm not sure why the list of activities helps her, because there are times she's on the wrong week, and yet she still comfortably refers to it. Perhaps it is knowing there is a plan, and that someone else is in charge or knows where she is, or maybe it is the activities themselves.

Our family has a lot to be thankful for. It has been a rough go, and there are worries on the horizon—the problems with Gummy's stomach are worse and likely side effects to her memory medicine, and we've had to stop them for a couple weeks to see if it'll get better. Life is never perfect. For this moment though, we're blessed with hope, joy, things to look forward to, and people willing to be there for Gummy.

Imagine how much more wonderful our world would be if we all had that.

chapter twenty-six

TAKEN

Probably the worst thing about dementia or Alzheimer's is that no matter what we do, it's not good enough. You can't fix it, or stop it from happening.

But we'll always have Paris.

Scratch that. I meant Thanksgiving.

Things have gone downhill since then.

Today hasn't been a good one, or yesterday. It's obvious that this disease is progressing with intensity. It's more than memory now; the disease is affecting Gummy's body.

I keep hoping that the incontinence and muscle weakness is a side effect of her medication. It's not looking good. She's off her medicine and nothing is getting better.

As we rush around getting ready for a Christmas Eve dinner with the family, including Gummy, Juan and I receive a call from assisted living. Gummy has called 911 on them to report her kidnapping, and gotten through. My determined mother-in-law had gotten ahold of the nurses' phone. When the staff caught her, she fought them off and barreled her way out the doors. They're locked electronically, so she must have hit them like a shot to break through. She raced down the hallway, the alarms went off, and half a dozen staff gave chase and intercepted her. This only added to her *Taken* scenario. By the time Juan and I get involved, Gummy has become hysterical.

Imagine for a moment that you've been kidnapped and are being held prisoner, and somehow you reach a family member by phone. Imagine the relief. Imagine you're hysterically sobbing out your fragmented understanding of your predicament, and they say, "Hey, Gummy-Gummy! I'm making you lobster for dinner!"

Yeah. It did not go over so well.

Juan and I juggle the phone, speaking alternately to Gummy and her kidnappers, negotiating ginger ale and making promises to come to her rescue. We are making little progress, so I call the doctor on Christmas Eve for help getting my terrified mother-in-law out of this particular hallucination.

Since this happened a couple hours before whatever time denotes the official beginning of Christmas Eve, I get some on-call doctor. With Juan still on the other phone calming his mother, I rush to give Gummy's medical scenario in a nutshell. She interrupts to ask, "Why are *you* calling me and not the nursing home?" This surprises me. I explain I'm the caregiver, and Gummy isn't in a nursing home. She's in assisted living. In memory care.

That doctor proceeds to tell me she isn't handing out drugs because she doesn't know me. She'll have to talk to the doctor at wherever Gummy is.

It isn't until I give up arguing and provide the number for the facility for her satisfaction that I realize she is suggesting that *I* want drugs.

It pisses me off. The thought process strikes me as exactly like the one that suggested I'd brought Gummy to the shire to get rich off her money. I understand this is the world we live in, but it still pisses me off. Don't ask me to have patience for being treated like the lowest common denominator. On top of that, memory care doesn't even *have* a doctor.

I stalk in circles in my kitchen muttering to myself, angry I can't get the help Gummy needs. Juan goes to rescue her from the kidnappers and I prep our holiday dinner, barely holding it together. After enough time has passed that the doctor should have called memory care, I call to see what, if anything, has happened. The on-call doctor had increased one of Gummy's medications, and ordered she be tested for a urinary tract infection. It is something, but it still angers me. My drug of choice at the moment is Christmas cookies, and I don't have any.

FOR CHRISTMAS GUMMY gets a Steelers jersey with *Gummy* on the back. She literally hugs it, and coincidence kindly provides a Christmas day game for her. This worked out even for those of us who don't care about football—for me that's writing time or naptime or plain old hide in my office and read introvert time.

By Christmas evening, sundowning opens the floodgates of *what the eff*, and Gummy is barely holding onto the laws of gravity. Despite the Steelers game, she sharks around picking up random items and goes into a two sentence loop.

Now who's taking me home?

Is this mine?

EVERY BIT OF this disease is Picasso awful. Everything is all mixed up. Relief and grief. Responsibility and guilt. Truth and lies. People with memory loss aren't the only ones wandering lost. The people who love them are too.

This week has again been a lot of Gummy time. She's not doing great, but the big problem is that she can't retain anything new. Period. She can't remember if she spent a day out with someone. She can't remember if she ate, or talked to someone, or took a bath. We don't even get Ten Second Tom. We get zero new data entered.

Gummy repels information.

In order to combat her Ninja tendencies and Mission Impossible escape attempts, she ends up being over-medicated a couple days. Remember the on-call doctor increasing one of her medicines? It's amazing how relief that the doctor is doing something often ends with an uh-oh. Even overmedicated Gummy is all *I will keel you*, but in horrifying slow-mo. The regular doctor immediately lowered her dosage.

She's often confused, sad, or angry, but perks up when we head out to do something. She's in her element at assisted living social functions and outings. The second these events end she can't remember they happened, and immediately drifts again. The longer she's left to drift, the worse it is.

Because of her murderous streak, Gummy has been talking to a psychiatrist. He's been going to see her every week since the evaluation I attended. She has decided he's a traveling preacher trying to get her right with Jesus. Gummy hides from him because she said she doesn't need those guys telling her how to pray.

It makes me laugh a bit. First, I'm pretty sure he's Jewish. Second, she says that he's been driving everyone crazy at her church since she was a kid.

We let him go today, even though he's a lovely gentleman. Insurance doesn't cover it and it's expensive and ridiculous. She can't remember their conversations. God knows what she's said to him, because I would stake my life on the fact that it's a bunch of codswallop.

This whole week has been consumed by Gummy stuff, all of which she cannot remember. She calls me all afternoon. It is different than usual. There is an underlying question every time: WHAT THE HECK IS GOING ON HERE? And HELP! I am thankful she knows she can call me and I'll tell her, but it doesn't stick. Nothing sticks. I was that person taking a personal call in line at the post office, and Target, and the doctor's waiting room.

Only someone at the doctor's office said anything. After hanging up I apologized and explained that my mother-in-law was being held hostage by kidnappers at the home she lives in, and I had to negotiate some ginger ale for her.

People are SO judgmental.

TODAY GUMMY IS watching football with Juan at our house. Between the game and the general confusion of dementia, she doesn't have a lot to say.

At one point she asks me for tweezers because she has hair on her lip. I offer to wax it off for her. One thing I've noticed about people is, no matter how bad off we are, we still want to look good. She agrees, and I take my mother-in-law into the bathroom and wax her lip. She's apparently never had it done before.

DAMN YOU!

We both crack up laughing.

Beauty is pain, Gummy.

I guess so! I didn't mean that, you know. It just hurt.

She allows me to proceed. I again tell her the story about cleaning the house of her own mother-in-law, when she went into a nursing home. I remind Gummy that she once made me promise not to allow her to get old and have unsightly facial hair. She has trouble following the story.

I can't remember anymore.

I know.

It scares me.

It scares me too. I can tell by looking at you you're sad. But you're not alone, you know. You have a lot of family who will take care of you.

I'm just noticing that.

I'm sorry you have to go through this.

I don't understand why. What is this for?

I don't know, but I want to ask you something, Gummy.

What?

I've been thinking about writing a book about this. About you and some of the things you've gone through with this memory problem. It would be funny, like right now, but sometimes sad too. Is that okay?

Yes. I'd like that. Make sure you say how good-looking I am.

TODAY I LEFT Gummy in Juan's capable hands. I have nine days until my current work in progress needs to get to the story editor. This little book *is* the story of our relationship, Gummy and mine. The whacked irony of not spending time with her so that I can write a book about spending time with her isn't lost on me.

It feels like when your kids want you to put together yet another Lego creation, but you ditch them in front of the TV because you're busy scrapbooking about family time together.

This story is both the easiest and hardest thing I've ever written.

Easy because all I have to do is tell the truth. Hard because all I have to do is tell the truth.

This is a person, a vibrant life, shattered and evaporating. Dementia is going to eat her like cancer, consuming not the body, but her essence, swallowing and terrorizing her. I'm not even certain what the family's job is here. To tell her it's okay, and watch? It's not fucking okay. I tell her that. It's not fucking okay, but I'll not leave you alone with it. If dementia covers your mouth, sucking away your words like your mind, I'll bear witness. I'll still see you. With a pencil and paper I'll capture a fragment of your light as I know it. Dementia can't stop me that. If someday it comes to exact it's revenge for the deed, I'll face him with the same words you have. Fuck you. Only you wouldn't say it like that.

Because that's not very ladylike.

GUMMY HAS BEEN calling me all day again. She can't remember why, and she sobs. She tries to gather her thoughts—injustices against the staff (they won't drive her home), people are missing (and she's fearful they died, but can't think who), and a general flat out terror that must surely be *normal* to have as all you've ever known gets erased from consciousness.

There have been times over the past centuries I've been married to her son that I've called her crying, and she's comforted me, commiserated, and even refused to give me one good reason not to strangle her son with my bare hands.

Now *that* is a good mother-in-law.

So I *am* both obligated and want to be there for her now. I do take time when I need to, and I make plenty of mistakes—the least of which is shutting her in the car door or forgetting her coat or purse, again.

This is a darkly human process, watching someone you love drift away, touching their hand, letting go, touching it, letting go, until one of you stops reaching or can't. I know that is what we're doing.

Tonight we are at the doctor's office so late that he walks us down the dark hallway and lets us out a back door himself. I admire the dedication of this shire doctor. They're going to start Gummy on a new kind of memory medicine tomorrow.

There is really no *good* memory medicine, but apparently all the drug companies are working on them and there is great hope for a good one. Gummy can't tolerate the popular one she's been taking. We're as sure as you can be that that drug is what has been upsetting her stomach.

In my opinion that drug really helped her memory. She started it in August, and managed to stick with it through Thanksgiving. By then she understood she was living in assisted living and would need to stay there for a while. She had her moments of discontent for sure, especially when sundowning, but for the most part she was doing pretty good.

Her stomach discomfort then got out of hand, and none of the medicine to counter it helped, so we had to take her off it. Perhaps it was coincidence, perhaps it wasn't. Her memory immediately shot to the point we suspect it would have been at if we'd never begun the drug.

Deterioration with dementia isn't reversible.

This is our new normal.

Gummy is declining physically; dementia is hurting her body and seeping her so deep in confusion she forgets to take care of herself, to move, to relax and breathe. When she first moved into assisted living, we always took the stairs or walked around outside. I can't remember the last time we took the stairs. She's fainted a few times now and often loses her balance. She's having trouble crossing her legs or even holding onto a Pepsi at the movie theater. During tonight's appointment, the dreaded beast *Alzheimer's* made a whispered appearance.

Classic Alzheimer's deterioration.

That doesn't mean it is.

We don't know for certain, and probably never will. It's all another boil on the beast.

As the staff at assisted living always say, "What's the difference?" Both Alzheimer's and dementia can deteriorate into physical symptoms. Memory loss by any name can stink as much.

It used to be that I slipped the doctor a note about what was really going on before we met, to ensure I never had to correct Gummy's fictional accounts of why we were there (hearing loss, itchy wrinkles, or pregnancy). Now I can sit beside her and speak baldly. Once or twice she'll look at me and say, "Really? I don't remember that." Mostly she isn't listening, or she thinks she's there with me and I'm talking about myself.

The latest CT scan of her head showed problems that I'm trying to work up the heart to research. Juan and I read it and kept right on moving. But every time we try to talk about it unexpected tears waylay me.

Despite the gaps in my understanding I've learned two things for sure about this disease. Dementia doesn't have a happy ending. And that is no freaking excuse not to love happily ever after.

We'll still do puzzles together. When someday soon I'm better at them than Gummy, I'll probably cry about it instead of happy dancing. Now we use paint pens and adult coloring books instead of ceramics, but I haven't entirely given up that hope. We'll still go to the movies, especially those Tuesday matinees where Gummy can talk out loud because no one else is there. With the fearlessness of a base jumper, she'll eat popcorn with butter and drink cherry Pepsi. If she wants pizza, she gets pizza. If she wants to go to the park and semi-stalk cute kids, she's getting that too. And if she wants to go home, well, she still can't have that, but I guess I'll just be glad she hasn't given up that dream.

chapter twenty-seven

HAPPY SMILEY

I t hit me as I sat in Gummy's room talking circles. She's like Happy Smiley all over again, and I killed Happy Smiley albeit with kindness, but he ended up dead all the same.

Gummy isn't the first time I've taken on an insurmountable task. Starting a business. Trying to single-handedly save the North American Monarch population. Writing novels in the uncertain chaos of today's publishing world. And Happy Smiley.

Gummy sits on her bed with her shoes on and purse in hand, ready to go home. She puts her hand over a belly swollen to such proportions her pants barely fit.

Does it hurt?

Not really. It's uncomfortable. I feel stuffed.

Me too. Gummy and I have both gained weight. Being a caregiver is a selfless job. I've been putting my things—good eating, working out, sleep—on the back burner for months now. It shows. Worse. I feel it. I keep thinking pretty soon I'll get in front of this, but I'm fully aware that I'm lying to myself.

I don't know why my stomach is like this.

I thought it was because of your first memory medication.

What? What are you talking about? What memory medication?

You were taking a memory medicine that seemed to upset your stomach. But you've been off it for a while now, and it's not getting better.

It's getting worse.

You're taking a different memory medicine now.

What? Nobody told me.

Today I brought her flowers. Gummy loves getting flowers, but flat out refuses to admit when they're dead. Since I brought yellow roses, I toss a dead poinsettia into the trash to make room. All that is left of it is an inch of stem and three shriveled crunchy dark leaves. She is not pleased. Her Amaryllis never bloomed because every time someone visits she yanks it out of the dirt and says, "What is this thing?"

Still, Gummy loves getting flowers, so we bring them.

I don't dare bring an orchid, though I know she would love one. You can't touch them. Skin oil makes the petals wilt. You can always tell when Gummy has been to my house by my orchids. She's very hands on.

Now look at this. What kind of plant is this?

Did you see this? Isn't it beautiful?

It doesn't really matter that she is tugging and patting it and therefore killing it. It's a plant. It distracts her for a moment. It gives her something to talk about. Something that won't freak her out. Once more I'm reminded to drop all expectations. That's the only way to survive this. Zero expectations. You don't get what you deserve. You get what you get. Deal with it. Don't take it personally. Make contact as much as possible. Expect nothing. Celebrate everything however miniscule.

Judging by that standard I should have brought an orchid. It would give her brief joy. You have to weigh things though. I try to put her first, but there are also limits. If it will bother me so much that I'll get short with her, or want to leave—which is happening more and more often—then I'll try to avoid it. Watching her kill an orchid would bother me almost to the same degree as the time I caught Gummy and Poppy letting my son *play* with minnows.

There is a huge difference between how parents interact with their children and how grandparents do. You can often spot kids being raised by their grandparents in a crowd. Sometimes grandparents will let them get away with things that their mom and dad wouldn't ever go for. Once I said to Juan that kids raised by their grandparents are weird.

You ought to know.

Touché, smarmy bastard.

The day of the minnows illustrates my thoughts exactly. Gummy and Poppy stood on the dock of a big pond, teaching my oldest how to fish with his little Snoopy fishing pole. At some point he got more interested in the bait than the fish. I think he was four. I'd only agreed to let him try to fish if they both watched him and he wore a life jacket—the matching Snoopy life jacket. It looked super cute. I heard him laughing and recognized that whacked laughter of kids up to no good. I went to investigate what was so dangerously funny. A couple minnows were flopping around the dock. Apparently one had gotten dropped and since it amused the little tyke, the grandparents provided a second when the first slowed his fatal flopping.

I lost my mama shite.

It's one thing to sacrifice live bait to the fishes for their dinner. It's another entirely to sacrifice any living thing for the amusement of another. Not even.

I publicly berated my in-laws and dragged my kid away for a good lecture. Juan later defended his parents to me.

They're a different generation.

They're so wild about this kid they'd let him juggle knives.

All of those things were true, but I was having no part of it.

It's often about how much you can handle. Can you deal with the hard stuff or does it cripple you? How well do you cope with anxiety? I'm pretty good with it as long as I can self-medicate with cookies and such. That is not a good thing. It could possibly mean I'm bad at it. Lately I've remembered it's absolutely necessary to put yourself first sometimes. It's not selfish to keep yourself alive and functioning. I know that, but sometimes I get so close to a problem that my face is metaphorically smashed up against the window and I stop seeing the big picture.

That is how I murdered Happy Smiley.

That damn bird looked like half a bald mouse with a few wet feathers. There is really nothing at all cute about a baby bird. It had fallen out of its nest. My niece named it Happy Smiley. It looked more like Sad Tears than Happy Smiley. The thing had pink translucent skin and sparse bedraggled feathers and if it had a half dozen siblings they might have filled the palm of my hand.

I was asked to babysit Happy Smiley for a few hours, and foolishly agreed.

You have to feed it every fifteen minutes.

Use this eye dropper. Just jam it into its beak and drop it down, one drop at a time.

Don't forget. You *have* to feed it every fifteen minutes.

It sounded doable. I could see its belly through its skin. And I kept track of the time meticulously. This happened before cell phones, so I couldn't text and ask if this was like pregnancy contractions. If it takes me five minutes to get the required amount of food in, do I go fifteen minutes from then, or fifteen minutes from when I started?

239

At first I wasn't certain, but I risked it and timed it from when I finished feeding him. He looked bad. Worse than when his rescuers had left. After a couple hours, I watched the clock obsessively. His little belly pooched out. It looked grey under the skin. Tight. Worrisome.

Do not die on my watch, sad little bird.

He did.

Happy Smiley passed onto the Great Nest in the Sky with a big, swollen, overfed stomach. Maybe it was only a little bird, just like the jumping minnows were only minnows, but I was responsible and had to own that. It bothered me.

Feeding something every fifteen minutes is a full-time job.

Caring for someone with dementia is a full-time job.

The legend of Happy Smiley has followed me over the years. I've learned to live with it.

Sitting here looking at Gummy's swollen belly brings it all back in a genuinely fearful way. In most ways she seems as helpless as that bird. Only this time I have no idea why that stomach is swollen. At least I'm not alone with it. The doctors are trying to figure it out too.

Lately Gummy's company has been trying to go visit her earlier in the day, because her memory is a little bit better then. One of my kids and I sneaked away from our jobs for a noon visit on Valentine's Day. She remembered him not his familiar face, but her connection to him. That usually doesn't happen. In her mind today she briefly connected the man with the kid chuckling over minnows and fishing with the Snoopy fishing pole.

We gave Gummy candy, chocolate covered strawberries, and yellow roses. It's probably too much sugar, and just too much. I need to institute a One Thing Policy when I visit. Two things are overwhelming. Three things send her into a tailspin. New stuff is hard for her, even presents. I slide the untouched strawberries into the little refrigerator we put in her room a couple months ago. It's stuffed full of everything we have ever put in it. She can't remember she has it. She has never taken one drink out of that little refrigerator. Every time I show it to her it is a shock.

If I hand her a drink from it, she holds it and asks twenty questions. When I explain the history of the little refrigerator, she says, "Nobody told me," and puts her drink back. Other days she refuses to touch anything inside, insisting that it is stealing and we will go to jail for taking a drink from the fridge.

Today she is calling me. She's also calling Juan, who is in Asia and fourteen hours ahead of our time. I had to call the assisted living switchboard so they would stop putting those calls through. You know what Gummy says when she calls you at three o'clock in the morning for a ride home, and you say you're in Asia? Nobody told me. Then she calls back in five minutes.

That phone might need to stop making outgoing calls sometime soon.

For a while Gummy enjoyed those Valentine flowers. Now I know she is wandering up and down the hallway with them, wondering where they came from. I will call her shortly and prompt her to open that little refrigerator and eat one of her strawberries. She will be shocked to find them. She will ask me how I knew they were there. And when I tell her that I put them there she will say, "Nobody told me."

chapter twenty-eight

IMAGINE THAT

What if today when you woke up you were in a strange bed? The first thing that seeps into your awareness is that the sheets on this bed are different. You open your eyes. This isn't your bed. This isn't your room. Maybe it looks vaguely familiar, like a room you were once in—possibly one from when you were a kid or in college. You can't quite place why it's familiar, but it is.

It's not the one you went to bed in last night.

Although, now that you think of it, you can't quite remember last night.

You get up and look for a bathroom. Afterward, you head down the hallway looking for someone or something familiar to try to make sense of this. Let's say that the one thing you can remember is that you're supposed to go to the store today. It's vitally important that you go to that store. Maybe, you reason, if you go to that store you'll remember what's going on. But you can't find your car keys. It hits you that you'll need your wallet or purse too, so you search and search for that. Eventually you find it. Now you have money but no car.

Starting to feel a bit anxious, you try to reason with yourself. You've always lived within walking distance to the store. If your car is gone, if someone borrowed it or something, you can walk to the store. You're going to walk it. That's reasonable, and obviously necessary.

You start walking. The street isn't familiar, but you keep going.

All you can do is keep going, hoping that something familiar isn't too much further.

You can't just stay in bed and wait.

So you keep going.

At the end of this street, when it seems time to turn onto another one and head toward what must be an area where a store should be, you hit another snag.

All the roads are wrecked. It's like there's been some sort of natural disaster and now you can't even walk along the roadway anymore. There's still that primal urge to get to civilization and do what you need to do, but how will you get there? You can't take the roads; they're destroyed and dangerous. You're going to have to strike out over the countryside. You're going to have to walk through people's yards and parking lots, maybe even creepy alleys, and possibly have to cross some streams. That nearby hill actually looks vaguely familiar—the one with a patch of pine trees on top of it. You don't know where you've seen it before, but you know you have seen it. Once you get up there, you might be able to figure out what direction to go.

For now you start walking through someone's backyard with an eye on that hill. Surely you'll recognize something soon. Maybe you'll even remember what happened and how you got here.

WHERE'S THAT CUP of coffee? Did you make coffee? Yeah, you made coffee…I think. Maybe that was yesterday.

You have a phone message about something important. You think it's from today. It was definitely this week. You told yourself to remember. There's going to be trouble if you forget. That much you do remember.

Did you feed the dog? He looks hungry, but he's got lying eyes.

Why is there a cat in your house?

Where's your car? Didn't the kids take it to the shop or something? You can't remember what shop, so how are you supposed to pick it up? It's been gone a long time, hasn't it?

Your kids come to visit. You can't remember if there are groceries to cook them dinner, but they want to take you out. That would be nice. You can't remember the last time you went out.

At the restaurant you realize your credit card is missing. The kids say they're treating you. More family shows up and you relax. When was the last time you saw any of them? It seems like a long time.

Your family is worried about your memory. You didn't mean to worry them. It's not that bad, you tell them. It isn't that bad. You're managing, and they have their own lives. You're the mom, you raised all those kids, cared for all those grandkids. Tell them you're fine. Use your mom voice. Don't let anyone worry about you. That's your job.

Someone told you that the kids are planning to take you to see a doctor up in the shire. They want you to pack your suitcase. You've got a doctor right here that you've been seeing for years. Why on earth would they try to pull this?

Tell everyone you aren't going anywhere. You'll go visit like you usually do, but you're not going to any new doctor. Do they think there's something wrong with you or something? The only thing wrong with you is your memory is getting bad, and that happens when you're old.

The kids help you pack your suitcase to go with them, and you're trying to remember what holiday is coming up. You're embarrassed to admit you can't remember. This seems like a weird time to go visit their house. Maybe you're going someplace else. Make a joke of it and ask. They answer, but you're tired, and you've already forgotten what they said. Ask again.

Now, where are we going?

To our house.

What? Why are we going clear to your house?

You're going to see the doctors there.

What are you talking about? I don't need to see a doctor. There's nothing wrong with me.

You have an appointment to have your memory checked.

Why did you come here? Where is this place? Is this the cabin? It looks different. Oh, look at the fox and bear. This must be the cabin. Is it fishing season? It must be if you're here. You really need to be getting home.

If you're at the cabin, why isn't Poppy here? That's weird. And if you're at the cabin, why is Saffi taking you to that church thing every day? That's definitely a church thing. They sing the same songs. How are you getting from the cabin to your church that fast? That used to be a long drive.

If you're at Saffi's house like she says, where's Juan? None of this makes any sense. This happens sometimes. You need to get home and rest, and everything will be clear again.

Why's your brother at the cabin? He never goes there. That's Poppy's family cabin. Why does your brother keep saying he's your son? What is he talking about? You haven't seen him in a long time well, maybe at Saffi and Juan's house in the shire. Why is he there? Why can't you figure this out?

If Saffi and Juan need to leave, why don't they just let you go back to your house? Why do they want you to stay in this room? You have your own house. They're not making any sense.

Who's renting this room for you to stay in? How much does it cost? You could go home for free. You're not staying here. You're definitely going home. You don't give a crap what's going on. You've had enough of this.

HAS A STINKY dog ever crawled onto your lap, leaving more fur on you than on his body when he scampered away? Have you ever loved someone without expecting anything in return? Love is messy and it makes your heart bleed, but that's no reason not to love. Nobody told me that, but Gummy showed me

Dear Reader,

It's the middle of the night. Most of this book has been written then, or gleaned from furious and desperate Facebook posts. I mined them for the progression of Gummy's story over the past year. Don't worry, my editor made me rework it into a real book and remove things like emoticons and hundreds of exclamation marks. I think she is going to allow a couple action designations. *Fist Bump* *High-Fives All Around* Purists must forgive. This book is a memoir, a personal note from me to the reader. Informality seems necessary.

Maybe the reader should be in the acknowledgements instead of here. There's no market for books about dementia, they say. It's too hard to deal with. Shalom, fellow doer of difficult things. *Low Bow* Thank you for reading against the current. If this book makes it off the shelves, it will be thanks to you.

I look forward to hearing your thoughts on Gummy's story. I also look forward to hearing the thoughts of other caregivers. We are legion, and we are tired, but I think we give each other strength. When we meet we share a common bond. Like the kids at Hogwarts who could see thestrals because they knew death. We've seen the cruelest of diseases, and wish only not to have seen it.

Hold onto your hope, no matter how bald and raggedy,
S.R. Karfelt

ACKNOWLEDGMENTS

Thank you to my Launch Team. Kelsey, Patricia, Kimberly, Barbara, Andrea, Katie, LaLa, Kathleen, Jan, Christine, John, Tom, Lisa, Laura, Ashley, Lori, Jennifer, Aleena, Colette, Holly, and Sarah. Thank you all for keeping me company in the void.

Thank you to my Facebook friends, for being the first ones to encourage me to turn my rants into a book. Special thanks to those who contacted me privately. To Barb for setting me down at Panera and encouraging me to do it. To Ruth for sharing Gummy's orange cookie recipe with the world. To Lisa and Katy, and so many others for sharing personal stories of dementia. I feel you. Thank you for being there.

For Julie and the creative well that is Women Reading Aloud, you lift and inspire me beyond words. That is saying something. Thank you, my kula.

To my editor, this is a big and special thank you. Bailey Karfelt, when you chose outside the mad scientist field for your college focus, I worried. You got sucked into it anyway, didn't you? Yet here we are, in the periphery of all that. A mother and daughter team. Writer and Editor. Who would have imagined? You, my clever, determined daughter, bled through this book as profusely as I did. I love you. On top of that, I respect you and your judgement. You ought to know, though, that I took screenshots of your smarmy editorial comments.

As always, my Dear Hubby, my Juan, deserves my thanks. This man puts up with my shit, and has for years. You're the wind in my sails, Juan, and always there when I need a gentle tug back to earth. If not for you, I suspect I'd wander aimlessly. When we brought Gummy into our home, you knew it'd be tough. When writing helped me put it into perspective, you trusted me with your heart once more. I hope you always will.

And, Gummy. Thank you for letting me share our story. If it didn't have dementia in it, it'd be perfect. Thank you for being there even when I didn't always want you to, for always taking the high road, for determinedly bridging the distance between mother-in-law and daughter-in-law, for eons of wise counsel, and for being my friend. (Thank you also for Juan. I know he's all your doing.)

DEMENTIA HOPE

Dementia hope is the thing with feathers
That perches in our soul,
And sings the song with the wrong words
And never stops at all,
And deepest in the fail it's heard
And soulless be the storm,
That could abash the ugly bird
That sings however shorn.
I've felt it in the coldest hand,
And heard it squall off-key.
Yet, never, thanks tenacity,
Will it ask the heart of me.

—With deepest apologies to Emily Dickinson

CPSIA information can be obtained
at www.ICGtesting.com
Printed in the USA
BVOW04*0754270517
485037BV00009B/9/P